This work: "A United Nations Renaissance", was originally published by Verlag Barbara Budrich and is being sold pursuant to a Creative Commons license permitting commercial use. All rights not granted by the work's license are retained by the author or authors.

AF716623

Cover Image Credit/Copyright Attribution: IIIerlok_Xolms/Shutterstock

John Trent/Laura Schnurr
A United Nations Renaissance

"*Politicians, pundits, and publics are moving inward and building walls whereas addressing global threats requires moving outward and breaking down barriers. More than ever, multilateralism is essential for problem-solving, and more than ever we need a fitter-for-purpose United Nations. Trent and Schnurr provide a persuasive and user-friendly introduction for a new generation of change-makers.*"

Thomas G. Weiss, Presidential Professor of Political Science, The CUNY Graduate Center, Past President International Studies Association

"*More than a simple forum or arena for confrontation of opposing interests, the United Nations must become an instrument for world governance. This excellent book, from Trent and Schnurr, goes a long way to push forward this idea.*"

Modesto Seara-Vazquez, Professor of International Organization, and Rector Oaxaca State University System, Mexico

"*The United Nations remains an essential global institution for advancing the values and practices of cooperation, development, and human rights, but it also needs reform; and especially it needs realistic proposals that give a way forward while still retaining and promoting the ideals of the Charter. This new volume places the UN in historical and contemporary perspective, identifies its critical strengths, challenges, and flaws in a balanced analysis, and suggests clear and constructive arguments and ideas for the changes that are needed.*"

Alistair Edgar, Professor of Political Science, Wilfrid Laurier University, Executive Director, Academic Council on the United Nations System

"The UN is being put to the test in today's jumbled and fractious global system. There is a foreboding over the growing trend among many member states including three of the permanent members of the Security Council towards anti - internationalist sentiments and the undermining of norms of global cooperation. As the title of this book signals, it is time for a UN Renaissance. This will only happen if there emerges a coalition of key member states, civil society groups, international institutions and good advocacy in the media and from the academic world.
This book makes clear why this is such an important cause for our time. And its focus on mobilizing young people to the cause is a worthy recommendation."

Lloyd Axworthy, Past President, University of Winnipeg, former Foreign Minister of Canada

"Global issues require well-functioning global institutions. The United Nations and it's agencies are critical global players that are needed more than ever given the increasingly interconnected world. The UN is vital in helping to create and support the right operating environment so that the Red Cross and Red Crescent and other organizations are able to fulfill their humanitarian mandates. Trent and Schnurr have written a concise and readable publication that should be read by young people the world over. It is hoped future generations would be encouraged to join the ranks in helping to rejuvenate an essential institution."

George Weber, Secretary-General Emeritus, International Red Cross and Red Crescent Federation; CEO Royal Ottawa Hospital

John Trent
Laura Schnurr

A United Nations Renaissance

What the UN is, and what it could be

© 2018 This work is licensed under the Creative Commons Attribution-ShareAlike 4.0. (CC-BY-SA 4.0)
It permits use, duplication, adaptation, distribution and reproduction in any medium or format, as long as you share under the same license,
give appropriate credit to the original author(s) and the source, provide a link to the Creative Commons license and indicate if changes were made.
To view a copy of this license, visit https://creativecommons.org/licenses/by-sa/4.0/

© 2018 Dieses Werk ist beim Verlag Barbara Budrich GmbH erschienen und steht unter der Creative Commons Lizenz Attribution-ShareAlike 4.0 International (CC BY-SA 4.0): https://creativecommons.org/licenses/by-sa/4.0/
Diese Lizenz erlaubt die Verbreitung, Speicherung, Vervielfältigung und Bearbeitung bei Verwendung der gleichen CC-BY-SA 4.0-Lizenz und unter Angabe der UrheberInnen, Rechte, Änderungen und verwendeten Lizenz.

Table of Contents

List of Illustrations

List of Abbreviations

CSR	Corporate Social Responsibility
DAC	Development Assistance Committee
DESA	Department of Economic and Social Affairs
ECOSOC	Economic and Social Council
ECOWAS	Economic Community of West African States
ESEC	Economic, Social and Environmental Council
FAO	Food and Agriculture Organization
FUNDS	Future United Nations Development System
G20	Group of 20
G77	Group of 77
G7	Group of 7
GA	General Assembly
GATT	General Agreement on Tariffs and Trade
GDP	Gross Domestic Product
GNI	Gross National Income
IBRD	International Bank for Reconstruction and Development
ICC	International Criminal Court
ICISS	International Commission on Intervention and State Sovereignty
ICJ	International Court of Justice
ICT	Information and Communications Technology
IDA	International Development Association
IDP	Internally Displaced Person
IFAD	International Fund for Agricultural Development
ILO	International Labour Organization
IMF	International Monetary Fund
IMO	International Maritime Organization
ITU	International Telecommunication Union
LGBT	Lesbian, Gay, Bisexual and Transgender
MDGs	Millennium Development Goals
MOOC	Massive Open Online Course
NAM	Non-Aligned Movement
NATO	North Atlantic Treaty Organization
NGO	Non-Governmental Organization
ODA	Official Development Assistance
OECD	Organization for Economic Development and Cooperation
OHCHR	Office of the United Nations High Commissioner for Human Rights
P5	Permanent Five, members of Security Council
R2P	Responsibility to Protect

RwP	Responsibility while Protecting
SC	Security Council
SDGs	Sustainable Development Goals
SG	Secretary General
UNAIDS	United Nations Joint Programme on HIV/AIDS
UNCTAD	United Nations Conference on Trade and Development
UNDP	United Nations Development Programme
UNEF	United Nations Environment Fund
UNEPS	United Nations Emergency Peace Service
UNESCO	United Nations Educational, Scientific and Cultural Organization
UN-HABITAT	United Nations Human Settlement Program
UNHCR	United Nations High Commissioner for Refugees
UNICEF	United Nations Children's Fund
UNIDO	United Nations Industrial Development Organization
UNIFEM	United Nations Development Fund for Women
UNODC	United Nations Office on Drugs and Crime
UNOPS	United Nations Office for Project Services
UNRISD	United Nations Research Institute for Social Development
UNWTO	United Nations World Tourism Organization
UPR	Universal Periodic Review
WFP	World Food Programme
WHO	World Health Organization
WMO	World Meteorological Organization
WTO	World Trade Organization

Introduction

Welcome to this short, analytical primer on the United Nations as it is and as it could be. It is short, because its first task is limited to only providing essential information about the UN. Analytical, because its second aim is to try to understand how we can think about global institutions. The United Nations is an international organization set up by a treaty between states in 1945 to help them cooperate on peace, development and human rights. Today the word 'international' has been expanded to become 'global', signifying that it is no longer limited to states but now includes other actors and activities beyond politics. We are witnessing the birth of global institutions whose task it will be to manage and govern the increasingly integrated global system. To understand the United Nations, we must understand its historical and global context and analyze its relationships with states, regional organizations, non-governmental organizations (NGOs), multinational corporations, and religious and cultural organizations. We must also study its strengths and weaknesses and its potential for the future.

Achieving the unthinkable

The world has never been a better place. We live in the most peaceful and prosperous era in human history. More than one billion people have been lifted out of extreme poverty in the past 25 years. From the early 19th century to the mid-20th century, the vast majority of the world's population lived in extreme poverty (Roser and Ortiz-Ospina, 2017). We have not experienced a war between major powers in decades. The majority of people live in democratic countries, compared to just over 10 per cent of the world population a hundred years ago. Technological advances have rapidly spread across the globe, with more people connected to one another and to information than ever before. Tens of millions of lives have been saved from small pox, polio, measles, malaria and tuberculosis, while HIV/AIDS infections and deaths have dropped substantially. More people have access to education and basic health care, and incomes in the developing world are rising.

We often forget this as we are constantly fed a stream of bad news from the media and from politicians eager to stoke fear and insecurity. We urgently need perspective.

None of this means we should sit back contently, satisfied with the headway we have collectively made. Climate change has exacerbated risks such as water crises, food shortages, social cohesion, livelihoods and security. Terrorism poses a very real threat to our security and stability. Intrastate conflict is devastating for individuals affected while also having regional and global consequences. We remain far from an adequate solution to the migration crisis caused by political and economic instability in the Middle East and North Africa. We need to respond rapidly when global pandemics occur, as they can spread like wildfire. There is no guarantee that we will avoid another global financial crisis similar to the one experienced in 2008-09.

The threats of our time are not like those of past eras that could often be solved by individual states alone or perhaps by a few states within a region. The diverse challenges we face today do share several common characteristics: they are increasingly complex in nature and they transcend national borders. Consider the hundreds of thousands of migrants and refugees who entered Europe in 2016 by crossing the Mediterranean Sea and arriving in Italy, Greece, Spain and Cyprus. Or the rapid spread of the Zika virus, which was confirmed to be present in Brazil in 2015 and by September 2016 had reached 48 countries and territories in the Americas and 10 countries in the Pacific, Asia and Africa (PBS Frontline). We know that the so-called Islamic State has developed a global network, to a great extent through social media, that has allowed it to recruit a large number of Western fighters to carry out terrorist attacks in cities like Paris and Brussels, while having branches around the world including in Yemen, Libya, Afghanistan, Bangladesh and West Africa. Similarly, climate change knows no borders; with rising sea levels, we have seen how carbon emissions in the one part of the world have threatened the very existence of island states on the other side of the globe.

These transnational issues require a deeper level of cooperation and coordination between states. They call for strong international laws and norms. Most importantly, they demand effective global institutions to develop and deliver coordinated responses. Yet few would disagree that such institutions remain a distant vision and that in its current state, the United Nations, the only international organization of its kind, is not up to the task.

So, with all this discouraging news, why did we begin this book on a positive note? The answer is simple: given the magnitude of our problems and the barriers we need to overcome, it is useful to remember that we have achieved incredible progress in recent decades—progress that previous generations would likely never have imagined possible. Just as we have surpassed expectations in creating peaceful continents and in advances in areas such as health, development and technology, we are equally capable of reforming the United Nations system so it is able to meet present and future challenges. Filling the emerging void in effective global governance will certainly not be easy, but history tells us it is possible.

The global governance deficit

How has the world changed since 1945? Has it changed to a degree which requires us to transform the international institutions that were created at that time? We argue that it indeed has. That our present challenges are as much global as they are national or local is a powerful rationale for improving our institutions, but it is not the only one.

The world is far more complex than it was during the post-war period. Some 51 countries came together to form the United Nations in 1945. Today, there are 193 member states. And great power politics have shifted tremendously since that era. Bipolar or unipolar global order has been replaced by one that is multipolar, with all that portends for instability.

When the UN was established, state governments were the dominant actors in the global sphere. While it may be too early to declare even the partial demise of the state-centric world, power is increasingly shared with other non-state actors, such as NGOs, foundations, multinational corporations, religious communities, regional coalitions or blocs, intergovernmental organizations, and groups of major economies such as the G7 and G20.

Economic, social and cultural globalization has meant that we are more connected than ever. Greater ease of transportation has facilitated global trade of goods and services. The same is true of the movement of people, resulting in rising migration and international travel. Rapid and complex communications provide new sources of knowledge and instantaneous access to information. Most people's lives have been affected by globalization in some way, but the extent varies significantly. And the gains from deeper integration have not been evenly spread; there are distinct winners and losers. Social and economic inequalities have reached new heights and capital is ever more concentrated in the hands of a few, with just one per cent of the world's population controlling more than 50 per cent of the wealth. The global society we live in today is by no means a global community.

By contrast, international institutions and their capacity for governance have not changed substantively. Established in 1945, the United Nations was designed for a different era. Its institutional structure and culture still reflect this past era, rather than the realities of the 21st century. It has not kept pace with rapid globalization and change. This stunted institutional development has led to its marginalization, with states looking elsewhere to solve the world's most pressing challenges. Observing this trend, many fear that the UN will slide into irrelevance unless it adapts to the times.

Sadly, at a time when we are in desperate need of greater cooperation and global governance, we are witnessing rising nationalism, xenophobia, and protectionism in many countries. Accelerated globalization and integration, which for decades were assumed to be unstoppable, are being met by a new wave of resistance; leaders and politicians favouring nationalism and isolationism over multilateralism are gaining support. We saw this when voters in the United Kingdom opted to leave the European Union in June 2016, and again less than five months later when voters in the US elected Donald Trump as their next President. The rise of nationalist political movements, on both ends of the political spectrum but particularly on the far right, is undermining international institutions such as the UN.

The United Nations' balance sheet

To properly diagnose what is wrong with the United Nations and what possible reforms could improve its ability to govern, we need to study its achievements and failures.

As this primer will explore, the UN has had numerous successes in its over 70-year existence. These range from the public achievements attributed to the UN, to the everyday governance that is rarely associated with it, to its effects which cannot easily be measured and rarely make headlines.

The contribution that the UN has made over its lifetime to creating a more peaceful, just and sustainable world is so immense that it would be impossible to cover everything. It has unmatched legal legitimacy and global convening power and has been indispensable in shaping international law, rules and norms through adopting treaties and other legal instruments. From the Universal Declaration of Human Rights in 1948 to the Treaty on the Nonproliferation of Nuclear Weapons in 1968, it is responsible for a considerable body of international law that guides states' behaviour. Several other treaties relating to the rights of indigenous peoples, persons with disabilities, children, refugees and other minorities have ensured that specific rights are outlined for individuals or groups that are particularly vulnerable. The UN has made real progress in tackling climate change between the Kyoto Protocol, the UN Framework Convention on Climate Change, and the Intergovernmental Panel on Climate Change. Most recently, the Paris Agreement succeeded in getting member states to commit to much-needed emission reductions. Beyond climate change, it has provided leadership on other environmental issues, from curbing ozone layer depletion, to protecting biodiversity and encouraging alternative energy.

While the UN cannot take credit for all the progress in socio-economic well-being and health, it has made enormous contributions. Its humanitarian programs deliver vital services to those in need, saving countless lives and improving the conditions of many more. It has been instrumental in shaping and implementing a global development agenda, as we witnessed with both the Millennium Development Goals in 2000 and the Sustainable Development Goals in 2015. The UN has done much to promote gender equality, including establishing key international norms and creating UN Women in 2010.

Beyond this relatively visible work, most international economic and political activity takes place fairly seamlessly thanks to a host of UN regulatory institutions. The result is that nearly all of us interact with the UN on a regular basis without recognizing it. Organizations such as the International Postal Union, the International Telecommunications Union, the International Civil Aviation Organization, and the International Maritime Organization are critical in a globalized world, yet we tend not to think of the UN each time we fly across a border, buy imported goods, make an international call or mail a postcard to another country.

Then there is the fact that the UN has been a stabilizing force contributing to global order for more than seven decades. It is the world's most important diplomatic forum. It has helped avert another world war, managed nuclear proliferation and helped prevent a nuclear weapons war, and reduced and ended internal and international conflicts through numerous peacekeeping operations and political missions. The nature of this work usually does not lend itself to public recognition. This is partly because we simply do not know what wars or conflicts have been averted due to the presence of the UN and its unending diplomacy, negotiations and mediation. Successful prevention rarely makes headlines as the absence of an event is unknowable and causality is difficult to determine. In the end, the UN is often taken for granted and does not get the credit it deserves, especially for its record in fostering peace and security. Nevertheless, it is worth remembering that without the UN the world would have to depend on increasingly brittle state-to-state relationships. Even with all its flaws, it remains far better than the alternative.

Despite all its achievements, even the most ardent supporter of the United Nations would not claim it is, or is even close to being, a perfect institution.

In the peace and security realm, the UN has been dealt multiple blows in recent years following a series of crises where it either failed to act or was bypassed altogether, along with a couple of highly publicized scandals. When the US and a few other states decided unilaterally to invade Iraq in 2003, they set a dangerous precedent in a world where only the Security Council was seen as capable of authorizing military interventions and the use of force. When the UN was not present at the 2015 negotiations on the Iranian nuclear agreement, it sent a powerful signal to the organization, which for decades has been pushing for nuclear disarmament and non-proliferation. For several years now the Security Council has failed to act in Syria, where a prolonged civil war has resulted in hundreds of thousands of deaths and the displacement of millions. The international community has tried to step in, but Russia and China have used their veto power to halt the attempts. The ability of the Security Council's five permanent members to veto resolutions helps explain why the UN is not always able to deal effectively with crises such as Syria. The UN's failure to counter the rising threat of terrorism has further damaged its image as the world's upholder of peace. On top of all this, reports of sexual abuses by UN peacekeepers in the Democratic Republic of Congo and Central African Republic along with findings that the peacekeeping force in Haiti was responsible for the cholera outbreak after the 2010 earthquake have together served to tarnish the reputation of the long-admired blue helmets.

On the human rights front, the UN has been inconsistent in its approach to dealing with grave violations and has let politics trump principled action nearly every time. This has severely affected its legitimacy and credibility as a human rights defender. It has proven unable or unwilling to prevent mass atrocities including genocide, crimes against humanity and war crimes, in Rwanda, Darfur, the former Yugoslavia, and Syria, among other places. At the same time, it has not been successful in coordinating an international response to the migrant and refugee crisis in terms of mobilizing the required resources and getting states to accept more people in dire straits.

The diffusion of the Responsibility to Protect norm has succeeded in making the principle of state sovereignty and nonintervention conditional rather than absolute. Yet politics and national interests still determine which situations will receive attention and which will be ignored. Meanwhile the International Criminal Court—a promising innovation created to prosecute the worst human rights offenders—struggles to remain relevant as some countries have chosen not to join while others are exiting.

The UN has had its share of troubles in advancing sustainable development too. The lofty goals set out in the post-2015 development agenda require far more resources than are currently available. At the same time, the complex UN development system made up of numerous organizations and agencies, often with overlapping mandates, has resulted in inefficiencies, duplication, lack of coherence and competition for scarce resources. Its standing as a global health leader has been jeopardized by its slow and inadequate response to pandemics such as the Ebola outbreak in West Africa in 2013-14, where its organizational culture was largely to blame. And the Economic and Social Council, the UN's principal coordination body for all economic, social and environmental matters, is in urgent need of reform.

With other regional and multilateral organizations, such as the World Bank and regional development banks, as well as private, philanthropic actors like the Global Fund and the Gates Foundation, being perceived as more efficient and responsive than UN agencies, the UN risks seeing development funding diverted elsewhere. Finally, as we look ahead it remains unclear whether it is fit to broker and manage 21st century partnerships for development that require deeper collaboration between public, private and civil society actors, while harnessing innovation and technology to enhance its development impact.

The urgency of current global challenges alongside the failures of the UN and the growing tendency for states to circumvent it suggest that action is needed now. There are a range of options available, varying from minor tweaks to the existing form and function, to rebuilding the organization from the ground up. If the latter were possible, the potential for a better global institution would be limited only by our collective imagination. But a healthy dose of pragmatism is advisable. We must recognize the hurdles that are to be surmounted; perfect cannot be the enemy of good.

Nevertheless, the demands on the UN system require more than a series of incremental improvements. The UN's structure, functions and allocation of resources have undergone reform over the years but not to the degree necessary to keep pace with rapid change. The organization today is not 'fit for purpose'. Yet there is no shortage of proposals for improving the dated institution. Scholars, UN officials and other experts are continuously developing workable reform ideas. Often, there is general consensus around what should be done. Though even in these cases, making change happen is no easy task for a host of reasons. When it involves a slow, bureaucratic and political organization like the United Nations it becomes harder still. Ultimately, no individual actor can do it alone. A concerted effort is needed to transform its institutional deficits. This could take the form of a multi-stakeholder coalition between willing states, NGOs, UN officials, independent experts, and other players. Now is the time to mobilize diverse actors, identify common goals and develop and implement an agenda for change.

Empowering youth

We equally cannot achieve the transformation needed without engaging youth. Home to 1.8 billion young people, the world has never in history had such a large youth population as it has today. One quarter of the world's population is between the ages of 10 and 24. Nine out of ten youth are in developing countries, many of which are experiencing a growing youth bulge while most developed countries tackle issues stemming from an aging population (UNFPA 2014). These young people, who are more informed, engaged and globally connected than ever before, should become the next generation of leaders who will shape our common future.

In his address to the 71st UN General Assembly, former US president Barack Obama praised the youth of our time, stating, "I have seen that spirit in our young people, who are more educated and more tolerant, and more inclusive and more diverse, and more creative than our generation; who are more empathetic and compassionate towards their fellow human beings than previous generations." He went on to say that because of young people's access to information about other peoples and places, they have "an understanding unique in human history that their future is bound with the fates of other human beings on the other side of the world."

Indeed, today's youth have incredible power to craft a more peaceful, just and sustainable world. The 2016 High-Level Segment of the General

Assembly saw an unprecedented number of world leaders acknowledge this, with 59 member states emphasizing the crucial role of youth in their national statements (United Nations Youth Envoy 2016).

The UN itself has taken note. In his second term as secretary-general, Ban Ki-moon made working with and for young people one of his top priorities. He established the Office of the Secretary-General's Envoy on Youth and chose Ahmad Alhendawi of Jordan to serve as the first-ever UN Envoy on Youth beginning in 2013. At 28 years old, he was the youngest senior official in the history of the UN. He was mandated to harmonize youth development efforts across the UN system, enhance the UN response to youth needs, advocate for addressing the development needs and rights of young people, and bring the voices of young people to the UN (Youth Envoy website).

Despite a series of public statements and gestures recognizing the immense potential of youth, there are too many young people around the globe who live in poverty and countless are being denied the opportunity to pursue their education and find decent employment. The number of children and adolescents out of school is on the rise, and reached 124 million in 2013. There are over 73 million unemployed youth worldwide. At 13 per cent, the overall youth unemployment rate is three times the adult rate, though it is even higher in some regions (in two thirds of European countries the youth unemployment rate exceeded 20 per cent in 2014; the figure is close to 30 per cent in the Middle East and Africa) (ILO 2015). The reality for girls and young women is even more troubling. Secondary school enrolment rates are often lower for girls than boys and only about two out of 130 developing countries have achieved gender parity at all levels of education. Unemployment affects young women more than young men in almost all regions, while in North Africa and the Arab States the female youth unemployment rate is almost twice that of young men (ILO 2016). Those in countries affected by conflict are also worse off than most.

Meanwhile, many countries are failing to give a voice to their youth; two out of three countries do not consult young people as part of the process of preparing poverty reduction strategies or national development plans (United Nations Youth Envoy 2014). Youth participation in national parliaments is low, with less than 2 per cent of parliamentarians globally under 30 years old (Inter-Parliamentary Union 2016).

It is little wonder, then, that, despite their potential, youth often feels disempowered. Voter turnout among 18-25 year olds continues to be lower than other age groups and a lack of civic engagement among youth is common. But young people cannot afford to watch from the sidelines. They need to press for action and positive change. They need to better the world for themselves and for future generations. With political rights come responsibilities. More than ever, the world needs its youth to elect good leaders, get involved in politics, expand their understanding of global problems and develop solutions.

Objectives of the primer

This primer on global governance and United Nations reform analyzes the organization in its current form while offering alternatives for the future. It aims to provide the fundamentals to those who are relatively new to the subject. It seeks to be informative and thought-provoking while remaining accessible to a broad range of audiences, varying from students to practitioners.

It is designed to:

- provide an overview of essential information about the United Nations system including its historical and global context;
- delve into the UN's record on its three 'pillars': human rights, peace and security, and development;
- introduce various ideas and proposals for renewing the organization so it can better meet the demands of tomorrow; and
- explore the role of norms, values and attitudes as well as diverse actors in building a movement for a UN renaissance.

We take the notion of renaissance to have two meanings. First, it is used to refer to renewal, rebirth, revival or even spring, which leads us to think about change, reform and transformation at the UN. The second sense refers to the essential meaning of the historical renaissance as 'a return to origins'. Dotted throughout the book are references to the UN's founding objectives, which included preventing the scourge of war, getting great powers to cooperate on essential decision making, striving to protect human rights, and ensuring economic coordination. This book is dedicated to a renewed search for the initial aims of the United Nations: peace, development, cooperation and human rights—and, indeed, much more as the world has continued to evolve. Thus, we use renaissance to call for a transformation of the UN that remains deeply rooted in its original lofty goals.

We hope this book prepares and inspires readers to join and expand existing efforts to achieve this renaissance.

Chapter 1 – Evolving International Organizations: the UN Past and Present

> *"[He] wondered why men could rarely harness this same sense of oneness toward good ends. Men would sacrifice their own interests, even their own lives, welding themselves together with bonds that far surpassed ordinary life, toward the purpose of killing one another. But when it came to creating beauty and life and love, too often men were left to act alone, their every act weighed against self-interest and simple inertia. If men were as good at creating heaven on earth as they were at creating hell, it would be a very different world."* Rachel Lee (2007: 474)

To really understand the United Nations it is not sufficient just to describe its structures, personnel and activities. It is first necessary to explain its beginnings and the intentions of its founders. And then the hard part begins: we have to weigh its strengths and weaknesses and analyze its components. This is the plan for this chapter.

Early international cooperation efforts

The United Nations is not the first but the third in a series of international organizations that date back to 1815. To give some historical context to the establishment and workings of the United Nations as it is today, the first part of this chapter describes these organizations and the key events that led to their creation (see Figure 1).

Figure 1: Evolution of international organizations, until 1945

The Concert of Europe

The Concert of Europe was founded by the Treaty of Vienna, which put an end to the Napoleonic Wars that had lasted nearly 20 years. In many ways it set the mold for its successors: the League of Nations and the United Nations. Like these last two, the Concert was founded in the aftermath of a devastating war waged by a group of allies to stop one nation from trying to set up an empire to dominate the world. The word 'concert' was intended to mean a bringing together of states in a concerted effort to work on common concerns. It was a radical departure from the past. At the time, it was called "a principle of general union, uniting all the states collectively with a federative bond, under the guidance of the five principal Powers" (Mazower 2013: 4). Up until the Napoleonic Wars, Europe (as other parts of the world) was ordered by an ever-changing "balance of power" by which each sovereign state attempted to maximize its own interests and stop any state or group of states from obtaining overwhelming dominance. This was the continually shifting basis of foreign policy. Napoleon's France had upset this balance. The allied powers wanted to re-establish it on a permanent basis.

Thus, the Concert of Europe was like a continuing coalition of the Great Power victors of the Napoleonic Wars (Russia, Prussia, Austria and Great Britain, plus the newly monarchical France). Its role was to convene meetings on a regular basis or upon need and to include other smaller countries to discuss overlapping interests and their efforts to maintain stable European relations. The Concert's two major functions were to maintain peace between countries and to ensure the internal stability of the established monarchical governments against nationalist, liberal and democratic revolts. Consultation often checked aggressive impulses. It generally achieved its twin goals for more than a half century from 1815 until the Franco-Prussian war in 1870-71.

The Concert of Europe sought to manage the affairs of the continent by binding all states to the rules of the international game. Sometimes this could only be achieved by intervening in the affairs of others. In fact, the word 'international' was a relatively new concept that suggested there were ongoing links between states despite their past habit of just wanting to 'do their own thing' based on their sovereign independence. This right of sovereign nationalism harked back to the 1648 Peace of Westphalia—which itself put an end to Europe's Thirty Years War. Nevertheless, on several occasions after the French Revolution, the Concert did not hesitate to interfere in the internal affairs of states to enforce a conservative restoration. For instance, in 1823 Concert members invaded Spain to drive a revolutionary government out of Madrid.

International relations grew slowly but steadily in the 19th century. Between 1840 and 1914, there were nearly 3,000 international gatherings. More than 450 international, private or non-governmental organizations were created and the Concert itself grew to 37 governmental organizations. International NGOs invited themselves to the international meetings, thus becoming new 'actors' in international relations and the forerunners of today's 'civil society'. Their 'competitor' was the historic notion of sovereignty (see Box 1).

Box 1: Understanding 'sovereignty'

Sovereignty grew out of the Peace of Westphalia of 1648 to define the legal identity of a state in international law. Each state is considered to have sovereign equality. There is a corresponding obligation to respect each other's sovereignty by not intervening in another's internal affairs. Internally, sovereignty signifies the capacity of the government to make authoritative decisions through exclusive jurisdiction within its territorial boundaries, which it has the right to defend. This is international law and its principles are hotly defended, but, obviously, it is not the international reality. The 'sovereign equality of states' is enshrined in Article 2.1 of the UN Charter. The principle of 'non-intervention' is to be found in Article 2.7. The 'right of self-defence' is embodied in Article 51. The UN Secretary-General has discussed the dilemma of the two concepts of sovereignty, one vested in the state and the second in the people and individuals. The *Report of the International Commission on Intervention and State Sovereignty* proposed the extension of the concept to include 'responsibility' alongside 'control', so that state authorities would have the responsibility to protect their citizens and would be responsible to the international community through the UN. This gave rise to the UN's 2005 resolution on the Responsibility to Protect (R2P).

Source: International Commission on Intervention and State Sovereignty, 2001: 12-3

Right from the beginning of international institutions, there was debate over how much the creation of a set of arrangements to maintain peace and stability could legitimize intervention in the affairs of others—debates which continue with the new UN policy of Responsibility to Protect (R2P). International affairs are not just about the arrangement of relationships. They are also about dominant ideas and a desire for power. So, it was said, "The Concert of Europe had not mastered the new art of international government; it was, on the contrary, a symbol of the very problems—autocratic leadership, bellicosity, an incomprehension of the values of freedom and the power of social change—that a true internationalism was needed to solve." (Mazower 2013: 12).

In reality, foreign relations in 1815 were really the playthings of sovereign monarchs and their aristocratic ministers who were determined that Europe would not only remain stable but would crush radical democratic tendencies. One example was the French Foreign Minister, Prince Talleyrand, who used his diplomatic dexterity to insist that France, although defeated, was too central to Europe to be dismembered. These men dominated the 1815 peace treaty, Congress of Vienna, and the Europe to which it gave rise. And they were only men because, with a few exceptions like Queen Elizabeth I, women were not involved in foreign relations until after the Second World War when Eleanor Roosevelt and several colleagues implanted the Universal Charter of Human Rights within the United Nations.

We can also recognize that international organizations are not purely political creations; they also reflect their time and their context. In many ways, politics follows the lead of economics and technology. Thus, the development of international organizations throughout the 1800s was greatly inspired by industrialization, and the expansion of railways and shipping beyond national boundaries. Business sought continent-wide security for markets and investments. Together, science and commerce framed the modern thinking that made possible the ideas of internationalism. Modern forms of trade and transport led to the forming of 'public international unions' (the forerunners of today's 'specialized agencies' at the UN) in the fields of transport, communications, weights and measures, statistics, patents, agriculture, labour, science, policing and sanitation. In addition, international movements for workers, women and peace formed world public opinion.

If fact, there have been a great number of influences on the development of international organizations. Although we recognize that the impetus for international organization comes out of the chaos of post-war disintegration, theorists maintain that, in general, an evolutionary or 'genetic' perspective seems best suited for us to understand how they developed from a host of interests (national and international, public and private), as well as internal learning processes and even the very act of international conferencing (Reinalda: 2001). Evidence suggests that in international organizations, innovation often comes out of lively and continuous debate originating in scientific, technical and humanistic communities (Reinalda 2001; Schemeil 2003). Indeed, the conferencing process creates a temporary equality among unequals and encourages the sort of open discussion that often gives rise to innovation (Murphy 1994: 62).

Conferencing was also conducive to developing the techniques and the psychological aptitudes required for successful multilateral negotiation (Claude 1966: 23). Engaged thinkers and practitioners found they could implement their ideas on a world scale and sometimes were called upon to prepare government positions. In other cases, NGOs learned that governments can be moved toward cooperation by private or unofficial pressures, when skillfully applied (Lyon 1963: 154). Changes in domestic politics such as new governments and political leaders can constitute windows of opportunity for new advances at the international level (Reinalda 2003: 9).

A note on the creation of the League of Nations

The context just described was both the process and the inducement for the forming of international institutions from the 1850s to the 1900s. It was also part of the background for the formation of the League of Nations in 1919 following the First World War. Other inducements were the atrocious loss of life, the destruction of countries, the wartime cooperation of the allies, and the need for an on-going organization as a forum to promote peace rather than war. Also of great significance was the spirited leadership of the American President, Woodrow Wilson. After the Second World War in 1945 it was much the same story that led to the United Nations except the leadership came from a new American President, Franklin D. Roosevelt.

The League of Nations was founded in January 1920 as a result of the Paris Peace Conference and the Treaty of Versailles which terminated the First World War. As the world's first permanent intergovernmental organization, its principle objective was to maintain world peace via collective security, disarmament and arbitration. It had an initial 44 state members, which rose to 58 in 1935. Its headquarters were established in Geneva immediately after its founding.

As we will see, the various in-depth analyses of the founding of the League and the UN teach us much about the causality, meaning and intentions of international organizations (see Mazower, Reinalda, Schlesinger, Archer and Trent). The League came about as a result of history, national interests, ideas, and personalities. It was a combination of 'big bang' politics responding to the war, and evolutionary development based on historical precedent. When it came to thinking about post-war institutions, the allied participants in the 1919 Paris Peace Conference (dominated by the US, France, Great Britain and Italy, with personalities like Jan Smuts of South Africa as additional players) had in their minds their cooperation during the war but also the internationalism of the past century. In their deliberations, they considered a number of options: resurrecting a new version of the old Concert; a model based on the American Monroe Doctrine which proclaimed US sway over Latin America; the British Empire transformed into a Commonwealth; and simply of a return to balance of power politics.

The thinking that predominated was essentially that of Great Britain and the US. Being great powers, neither wanted any new arrangements to tie their hands too much. They wanted to maintain the Anglo-American alliance but in a larger format that did not look too self-interested or racist. The French and the British did not want the League to interfere with their imperial ambitions. Many thought the new arrangements should be as light as possible and be centred on negotiations, international law, mediation and arbitration. For both the League and the UN, the wartime experience of cooperation was crucial as a seedbed for more centralized and systematic world relationships and the importance of procedure and precedents.

But when push came to shove, it was the negotiations between the leaders of the major, victorious powers which drove the founding of both the League of Nations and the United Nations. In Paris in 1919, U.S. President Woodrow Wilson ended up in protracted negotiations with the French President Georges Clemenceau, British Prime Minister David Lloyd George and Italian Prime Minister Vittorio Orlando—leaders who were equally creatures of their own personalities, philosophies and visions, and influenced by their close advisers. Known as the 'Big Four', these leaders had no intentions of relinquishing control of the conference agenda—a tradition that is maintained to this day.

They also maintained the earlier tradition of diplomatic secrecy because they thought not to do so would be "a veritable suicide" for their negotiations. But they surrendered to the growing demands of journalists for regular plenary sessions and briefings. Small states were "given something to do" as an addendum to the Council and in the powerless Assembly. Following the submission of plans by various leaders, thinkers and associations, Robert Cecil, the British undersecretary of foreign affairs, was able to provide a draft text for the League, based in part on a study of historical precedents (as the American Secretary of State later did for the UN). It was discussed, amended and adopted in two months. However, it would be incorrect to think there were no other significant influences on the peace negotiations. Among the other major influences were: the blending of morality and realpolitik in the provocative ideas of Jan Smuts, Prime Minister of South Africa; the London intellectual elite including Leonard Woolf, who had written a suggestive book entitled *International Government*; the demands of small allies, especially those in the nascent British Commonwealth who had helped win the war; and popular associations (now NGOs) such as the League of Nations Association.

The League of Nations as an institution

To the degree that he wanted a permanent organization, President Wilson of the United States wanted to keep power with the politicians in a forum for quasi-parliamentary deliberations rather than with the lawyers in a sort of super judicial court. He wanted an institution that would evolve with the collective will. He also wanted to protect the territorial integrity of the growing number of nation-states in a universal association of nations capable of acting in the common interest to help prevent war. "The days of the Treaty of Vienna are long past," as British Prime Minister Lloyd George put it, referring to the birth of the Concert of Europe (Mazower 2013: 127). There were, of course, many contradictions. The general principle of national self-determination remained vague. Britain, the great imperial power, thought that the Empire itself resembled “a league of nations”. Prior to the Paris Peace Conference, many questions remained. How much executive power would a League possess? How far would it be committed to protect established boundaries? Could sanctions be automatically triggered? How far would the League go beyond being just a more permanent conference system?

However, history shows that once at the Peace Conference, personal diplomacy took over. A committee chaired by Wilson rapidly approved the British draft agreement. There would be a tripartite division of powers in a parliamentary type organization. It consisted of: a Council with Great Power permanent members and four elected, rotating lesser powers in a sort of ‘upper chamber’; a one-member, one-vote Assembly; a relatively weak secretary-general in an administrative rather than a diplomatic post; and, in 1922, a Permanent Court of International Justice.

The Council’s permanent members were France, Great Britain, Italy and Japan (the US did not join). Eventually, the Assembly’s 40 members, meeting at the new headquarters in Geneva, represented minimally the various parts of the still-colonized world. Almost all of Africa, Asia and the Middle East were controlled by European imperial powers. The Assembly had no law-making functions and each member could veto any action. In any case, the League lacked any standing forces or mechanisms for enforcing peace. All it could do was to recommend arbitration, sanctions and boycotts. It was even unable to apply sufficient pressures in clear-cut cases of aggression. Nevertheless, it did introduce a democratic dimension of public deliberation and opinion. Also, the full Assembly only met once a year, so the rest of the time the League’s merit-based civil servants were free to take the initiative.

This became a major dimension of the League and its definitive heritage. The bureaucracy was created by Eric Drummond, a mid-level official of the British Foreign Office, who went on to hold the office of Secretary-General for 14 years, longer than anyone either at the League or the UN. Having built a small (650), highly professional international civil service, one with permanence and autonomy that favoured expertise over diplomacy, he became one of the architects of modern international organizations. It was divided into functional secretariats that “cemented the connection between internationalism and technical expertise” (Mazower 2013: 148). For instance, German and Soviet officials worked with the League’s technical services before their countries even formally joined. The Secretariat also took advantage of Articles 23 and 24 of the League’s Covenant which gave it wide responsibilities and allowed it to become an umbrella organization that gathered under its auspices the 31 international bureaus (also called ‘permanent conferences’ or ‘public international unions’) that had been formed before the First World War.

One example of the League’s extraordinary feats as a humanitarian organization was its overseeing of emergency relief camps giving succour to the Russian, Armenian and Greek refugees in the Balkans in the early 1920s. They ran and financed tented encampments and brought in health experts to stop infectious diseases. They helped the Greek government get loans to resettle hundreds of thousands of refugees. They created the Refugee Settlement Commission to build new settlements, even small towns. This effort by a government organization was entirely new. It had previously been the work of charities. We can easily see how there is an eerie resemblance to events in the Middle East since 2010 and may ask: why is the world still having to deal with the same horrific problems one century later?

The League also became recognized for gathering data and issuing volumes of statistics. Its health, transport, and financial and economic sections became indispensable in the interwar years. Strangely enough, many of its personnel came from the United States and much of its technical funding came from the Rockefeller Foundation. It worked hard to restore monetary stability but lost out to the protectionism of the Great Depression. Its members prided themselves on being impartial and above national interests (unlike the UN) but not above paternalistic interference in member states' internal affairs. Overall, some two hundred employees of the League's Secretariat went on to work for the UN and even to be leaders of a number of post-Second World War international organizations—including Jean Monnet, who would become one of the founding fathers of the European Union.

That said, the League was battered continuously by horrendous public calamities, the defection of prominent members and the battle of ideologies. In 1918 and 1919, Spanish influenza affected one fifth of the world's population and killed between 20 and 40 million people, exceeding the deaths during the First World War. More deadly than the Black Plague in the 1300s, it was the worst scourge ever to sweep the world. But the League also had to face continuing war and a refugee crisis in the Middle East, economic collapse in Eastern Europe and a public health disaster including influenza, typhus and mass starvation. In addition, Western leaders were terrified by the spread of communism from Russia's revolution, which was welcomed by many in Western Europe due to economic collapse and massive unemployment. On top of all this, the new League was called upon to administer the territory of the Saar and the Free City of Danzig and look after the plight of the Christians in Turkey and the status of Armenia. By 1929, the world fell into the grip of the Great Depression.

The defection of prominent states never ceased. Perhaps the cruellest blow to the League was the vote by the U.S. Senate against joining President Wilson's brain-child. The decision reflected a refusal by part of the political elite to become enmeshed in 'entangling alliances' and the world's troubles. Public support for the League was low, and there was resistance in Congress to making commitments to international organizations that would hamper the freedom of action of the United States. It was a fine example of American isolationism—something that still lingers today. But it was paired with a will to international leadership, exemplified in the interwar years by the private endowments which financed support for the League and for institutes, journals, international relations clubs and conferences to train Americans for their role in the world.

For its part, the Soviet Union did not even join the League until 1934 and then was the only state to be kicked out after it invaded Finland in 1939. Germany, which had not been welcomed at the beginning, joined in 1926 and then withdrew under Hitler's Nazi regime in 1933. Mussolini's fascist Italy followed in 1937 after having invaded Ethiopia. Japan, unhappy with criticism of its occupation of Manchuria, withdrew in 1933. Germany, Italy and Japan, which would become known as the Axis powers, each had a grudge against the dominant colonial system the League represented. They wanted what the French and British had. They wanted territory, colonies and power. For them there was a power imbalance in the world represented by the League. This virtually left Great Britain and France among the Great Powers and they were still too ravaged by their losses during the First World War to devote energy to saving the League. What with its heavy burdens and quarrelling members, the League was not able to stop the slide to a new world war.

The battle of ideologies consisted mainly of multiple attacks on the Western theoretical claim about the fairness of international law, equally applied to equal states, as a keystone of the League. For instance, the Western empires did not even subject themselves to minority rights treaties. What Germany, Italy and Japan had in common was their criticism that the League was just a 'fig leaf' to keep in place a territorial status quo that favoured Great Britain, France and the US. The same criticism was to be levelled later about the UN. Hegemony, the leadership of one or more states, was the central German conception of world rule. Japan too saw the League as protecting the self-interests of the imperialists in Asia.

The Soviet Union weighed in with the establishment of the 'Third International' in 1919 as a direct rival to the League of Nations. Lenin even referred to the League as a "stinking corpse" (Mazower 2013: 177). Soviet diplomats became more measured and conciliatory though, even joining the League in 1934. For Moscow, its security came before revolution. For its part, Italy promoted a 'fascist internationalism' in a fascist European confederation, supposedly fighting for the rights of European nation-states.

One can see arising out of these affirmations of sovereignty and nationalism the destabilizing potential from which the UN too would suffer. The leading American political scientist, Quincy Wright, worried that, "totalitarianism has unmasked the inadequacy of the philosophical and political foundations of international law." (Mazower 2013: 187). Its impartial authority lay in tatters. International law would require a demonstration of shared values and interests, alongside the enforcement capacity.

Box 2: Strengths and failures of the League of Nations

- The quasi-parliamentary model at the League's core was abused from the start by members who came to Geneva more for theatrics than policy-making. The pre-war ideals of open negotiations and diplomacy to stimulate world public opinion ended up creating unfulfilled expectations.
- The unanimity rule (i.e., each member holding a veto) made decisions hard to reach, thus condemning the organization to impotency.
- Its irresolution was magnified by its lack of any means of enforcement or deterrent such as armed forces or a police force so that even the rules and laws it did proclaim lacked authority.
- The League was operating on a shoestring in a period of financial stringency. Its budget of $5 million a year was less than a thirtieth of the UN's—also considered minuscule in today's multi-billion-dollar world.
- Due to these failures, the League was not able to provide answers to the urgent crises of the day, thus reinforcing public perceptions of its inefficacy.
- The League's technical services provided by its professional civil service took international humanitarian cooperation and the promotion of science much further than anyone had imagined possible before the First World War. It offered the promise of democratization and social transformation through technical expertise.
- Its technical, intellectual and scientific skills proved the value of an international organization. Even if it was a diplomatic failure, its expertise and international action became a model for the evolutionary growth of cooperative behaviour due in part to its flexibility and multitasking.
- Not all initiatives worked out. For instance, the Institute for Intellectual Cooperation had few tangible results as Europe fragmented ideologically, and few states ratified the 1937 Treaty for an International Criminal Court (60 years before its time)—even the French proposal for a federal union of Europe to combat the Depression was not successful!
- The League's enduring influence was as a vehicle for world leadership based on moral principles and the formal equality of sovereign states. It managed to marry the democratic ideal of a society of nations with the reality of Great Power hegemony.

We recall all this (along with the League's strengths and failures outlined in Box 2) now to remind ourselves of the sensitivity of international organizations to the politics of their member states, and to the continuous attacks by ideologues, by the media and by an unreasoning public.

From the League of Nations to the United Nations

One day during a visit to Washington in 1941, Prime Minister Churchill was just getting out of his bath when President Roosevelt rolled his chair in and declared that he had thought of the perfect name for the new organization: the United Nations. Churchill immediately agreed it was a brilliant idea (Mazower 2013: 197). It is little known that, although the UN was not officially founded until the San Francisco Conference in 1945, the Second World War was fought under the auspices of the United Nations Alliance in which 26 allies joined the United States and Great Britain. With their backs to the wall, the war years were in many ways the heydays of liberal multilateralism and institution building. The war encouraged cooperation. In terms of international relations theory, we may conclude that building the UN was evidence that multilateralism and robust intergovernmental organizations were viewed as "realist necessities, not liberal window dressing" (Plesch & Weiss 2015: 199).

In 1942, the UN Information Office went to work and the Food and Agriculture Organization (FAO) started planning for the eradication of hunger. Aside from the many backroom debates about the nature of the UN, the UN Relief and Rehabilitation Administration was created in 1943 (it then shut down operations in 1947). The International Labour Organization was revived in 1944, the same year that saw the Bretton Woods UN Monetary and Financial Conference that gave birth to the World Bank Group and the International Monetary Fund. The UN War Crimes Commission was a precursor to the Nuremberg and Tokyo trials. In a strange little twist of fate, one of the remaining utilities of the League of Nations was transferred to the United States in 1941. With the help of the Rockefeller Foundation, 12 key Secretariat members with their files and experience transferred to Princeton, New Jersey to take up residence in the Institute for Advanced Study where they advised on the post-war problems.

So, what was behind all this creative action? What did the leaders want out of the new United Nations? Needless to say, they all wanted an organization that was strong enough to promote international peace. In addition, Great Britain wanted to maintain its 'special relationship' with the US. It also believed that having the US and the Soviet Union in the new organization was more important than the exact form it would take. Joseph Stalin, the leader of the Soviet Union, wanted to maintain the alliance until he had time to rebuild his country. U.S. President Roosevelt had learnt from his 'New Deal' economic development program that good politics went hand in hand with socio-economic programs. In the context of the UN, this meant that fostering post-war, international economic and social stability would make a contribution to maintaining peace and security. The massive unemployment following the First World War led to social unrest that was a harbinger of a new world conflict. The Americans thought it was crucial to prevent a renewed post-war economic slump by structuring an international bank and monetary fund to slay the triple-headed dragon of economic nationalism, speculative capital flows and trade barriers. To determine where they were heading, the Americans set up a top-secret 'Division of Special Research' as early as 1941 under Leo Pasvolsky, an aide to Secretary of State Cordell Hull, to plan a new permanent world organization.

The three major allies (Britain, the Soviet Union and the US) had differing ideas right up to the last minute, even concerning the actual nature of the new organization. Early on, they envisioned an international police force run by the three allies along with China. Another option considered was to set up a 'World Council' made up of three regional councils (Europe, the Americas and the Pacific). In the end, they agreed to some post-war structure that could more effectively manage conflicting interests and contain, at minimum, the threat of military and humanitarian disasters (Meacham 2003: 202-29).

By the Dumbarton Oaks conference in 1944 and the Yalta conference in 1945, the concept of the United Nations started to gel. The conversation shifted from regional councils and other proposals to planning for an organization that could exert force to try to maintain order, complete with a Security Council (with permanent members) and a General Assembly (ibid: 321).

It was decided that the UN would preside over a vast expansion of the social policy initiated by the League Secretariat, and that a voice would be given to the smaller nations under the leadership of the major powers. Churchill and Roosevelt sought to build institutions that would prevent the mistakes of the first half of the 20th century from repeating themselves in the second half. Nothing was left to chance as the Americans ramped up the promotion of the United Nations ideal using not only bipartisan political resolutions but advertisements, Hollywood showgirls, and musical anthems. On March 1, 1945, just weeks before his death, Roosevelt made a last plea for a global, rather than regional, organization. He told Congress that the UN agreements in Yalta "ought to spell the end of the system of unilateral action, the exclusive alliances, the spheres of influence, the balances of power, and all the other expedients that have been tried for centuries—and have always failed." (ibid: 321).

What we can see from all this is that states only began thinking about international institutions when they feared their interests or those of the world were in danger. It was major powers and their top leaders who set the rules, exploring numerous concepts and taking nothing for granted at the outset. Smaller countries were marginalized in processes that were neither inclusive nor democratic. Concepts and details would be forged by some 'secretariat' in the background for debate by the leaders, who in turn would work through the issues and come to conclusions that shaped the future. This particular lesson should give us hope for change. As Plesch and Weiss concluded, "We thus should not act as if today's international political order were immutable or pre-ordained. The 1940s should give us the courage to formulate ambitious visions about improving future world orders." (2015: 203).

From the experience of these three international organizations we should recall the following:

- All resulted from efforts to create stability and peace after devastating wars;
- They also resulted from the evolution in international relations and the socio-economic context;
- All were dominated by the great powers of the period;
- Foreign relations are still masterminded by political elites with little democratic control;
- The right of international political intervention is still contested;
- All were torn by the contradictory desires for both cooperation and sovereign independence, and for equality but also leadership of the strong;
- States want the help of international organizations to smooth out their relationships—but these organizations are to be the creatures of the states and must not become too powerful or independent; and
- International organizations are not purely political creations; they also reflect their unique context.

Introducing the United Nations

The United Nations was founded at the San Francisco Conference in 1945 by delegates from 50 countries (Poland did not attend the Conference but signed the Declaration later that year, becoming an additional founding member). The overall design of the United Nations had much in common with its predecessor, reflecting how international institutions tend to evolve rather than change rapidly. Illustrating the continuity between the two organizations, few people even noticed that the United States joined the League *after* the Second World War, a year before it was legally wound up at a final ceremony in Geneva in 1946.

As with the League, the UN is based on a tripartite parliamentary structure including a Security Council (as a sort of Cabinet), a General Assembly or debating chamber with one vote for each state member but with few powers (sort of like legislatures), and an administrative Secretariat and secretary-general who, once again, is more secretary than general (a prototype of a public service). Likewise, the International Court of Justice in The Hague (replacing the Permanent Court of International Justice) can only accept cases submitted to it by members and its decisions are more recommendations than orders. Also, the UN has no prosecutor, no police and no jail. And once again, although the UN Charter speaks glowingly of fundamental human rights and it gave birth to the Universal Charter of Human Rights, there are no binding obligations that commit members to protect citizens—even if they sign treaties to do so.

There are also significant differences between the League and the UN. The very powerful Security Council was designed to take action whenever its members are in agreement. Vetoes were accorded to the Great Powers (the Permanent Five members) to make sure they do not have to leave the UN to protect their interests—which was one of the downfalls of the League and something we must remember when we discuss criticisms of the veto later. No other members were given veto power with which to block action, so there is no proto-anarchy as in the League. The Security Council is given exclusive jurisdiction over maintaining peace and security. Various chapters of the Charter give the Council gradated powers to enforce the peace, starting with investigations and moving on to negotiations, sanctions and eventually a possible call on all countries to protect the peace of the world. There were also provisions for armed forces and a command system, but when the Cold War started soon after the founding of the UN, these were never acted upon.

Another new feature was the Economic and Social Council, which was intended to spearhead much broader development and cooperation of experts than imagined under the League. As we saw, because of his experience with the New Deal to help overcome the worst aspects of the Great Depression, this had become one of President Roosevelt's main goals. Thus, the UN combines humanitarian technocracy to promote economic and social development with the powerful potential of the Great Powers to protect the peace whenever they can jointly decide to do so. After more than 70 years, it can be claimed that the UN has kept the major powers together—and talking, not fighting. Some say it was the rebirth of the League, only with more teeth and with the participation of the United States.

The principal organs of the United Nations

The Security Council

The Security Council is formed of five Permanent Members (the P5) wielding vetoes (the United States, Great Britain, France, Russia and China—the victors in the Second World War) plus, currently, 10 other rotating members elected by the General Assembly for two-year terms. It is the UN's most powerful forum. The rotating members represent the various regions of the world. Each member has one vote. Procedural matters require nine votes. Substantive matters require nine votes and the absence of a veto. Thus, in theory the rotating members have a negative or blocking vote for stopping things from happening—it is sometimes referred to as the 'sixth veto'. The presidency of the Council rotates monthly among its members.

The Council bears the primary responsibility for the maintenance of international peace and security. Linda Fasulo has provided an excellent word portrait of its powers: "It has the authority to examine any conflict or dispute that might have international repercussions and to decide matters affecting the fate of governments, establish peacekeeping missions, create tribunals to try persons accused of war crimes, apply economic sanctions to misbehaving governments, and in extreme cases declare a nation to be fair game for corrective action by other member states. It is the only UN principal organ whose resolutions are binding on member states, which means that governments do not have the option of choosing which of the council's decisions they will or will not accept and help implement." (2015: 55).

The role of the UN in peacekeeping and peace enforcement (under Charter Chapter VII: 'Action with regard to threats to peace') has increased immeasurably since the first United Nations Emergency Force was deployed for the Suez crisis of 1956. The UN went from modest monitoring and supervision operations in the 1940s, to now supervising more troops in the field (contributed by members) than any country. By 2016, there were 16 UN-led missions in the field for an annual cost of some $8.2 billion (on top of the regular UN budget). They include large civilian and police components. In the post-Cold War period after 1990, the P5 in the Security Council were much more cooperative and were willing to tackle more numerous and diverse conflicts including domestic rivalries. Often this has led to a need to work cooperatively with regional partners in 'coalitions of the willing' from such groups as the North Atlantic Treaty Organization (NATO), the European Union, West African States and the African Union. The Security Council now goes well beyond pure peacemaking to work toward peacebuilding with the monitoring of elections and long-term international support for the development of institutions and finances. There has also been a reinforcement of combatting terrorist threats.

Aside from peacekeeping, the Security Council has at its disposal a whole series of measures it can use to try to change the orientation of 'misbehaving' states. One of the most dramatic forms of influence is sanctions that can be used to restrict the movement of finances, weapons, trade, travel or diplomatic contacts. As will be discussed in the following chapter, sanctions have become more targeted and efficient over the years in response to criticism and there have been several examples of successful use.

The number of formal and informal meetings of the Security Council has fluctuated over the years. For instance, there were 117 in 1988 and 373 in 2012. Under pressure from Canada and other members, the Council has slowly evolved to a more open process beyond the meetings of diplomats of its 15 members. It now invites non-members, UN officials and agencies, and even international NGOs. It also consults with states making major contributions to peacekeeping and other UN operations. The Council has also established some 40 subsidiary bodies to monitor specific places or issues. Over the years, the Security Council's agenda has broadened to include not only peacekeeping but also humanitarian concerns, the international right to intervene, the plight of war induced refugees, monitoring of elections, post-conflict peacebuilding, terrorism and the creation of international criminal tribunals.

The question of the veto power afforded to the Permanent Five is highly significant both for the nature of the UN and its future. The major victorious powers insisted on having a veto in the new international organization in order to protect their 'vital interests'. Other states went along with it to ensure the presence of the major players and make sure they did not leave at the first hiccup. However, it was never thought the P5 would use the veto or the threat of a veto to cover their whole foreign policy, as has often been the case, most recently with Syria.

Russia has long considered Syria to be in its 'sphere of influence'. China on the other hand has no clear connection with the Middle East. Yet both have used their veto power to block resolutions to halt the Syrian civil war, on the basis that *may* interfere in their internal affairs or *may* establish a principle or a pretext for such intervention. In particular, they fear the aggressive overreach of the 'Western powers' (the US, Western Europe, and their NATO allies). In 2007, Russia and China accepted that NATO, on behalf of the UN, could use the Responsibility to Protect norm to authorize air support to protect the civilians and the rebels against Gaddafi in Libya. Western powers went far beyond this mandate though, by instituting a complete regime change. So, Russia and China feared that even having the Security Council authorize 'no-fly' zones over Syria would be the thin-edge-of-the-wedge to permit the complete overthrow of the Assad regime. They considered that stopping such a precedent for intervention in domestic affairs is vital to their interests and worthy of a veto—however hard it is for the rest of the world to understand because it permitted this deadly war to continue for six years.

Given this situation, many critics have called for the complete abolition of vetoes in the UN. Meanwhile, those who think the P5 will never let go of their advantage propose that the world work toward a curtailment of the veto so that its use would exclude resolutions dealing with war crimes and be limited strictly to resolutions directly affecting the vital interests of a P5 state.

Another basic problem with the current Security Council is that it is not representative of the world to which it is supposed to give leadership. This has led to calls for the expansion of its membership, for which there has already been a precedent in 1965 (one of the few amendments of the UN Charter). However, this too is deeply political and the debate has been ongoing for decades. Various proposals for reforming the Security Council, specifically those dealing with the issue of representation, are discussed in Chapters 2 and 5.

In sum, the Security Council can be very effective at protecting international peace and security when its members are able to work together. Since the end of the Cold War, it has proved influential and even transformative as it has asserted the UN's responsibility to intervene, even in internal conflicts. Yet it has crucial shortcomings, including its occasional failure to act, its unrepresentative nature and its two-tier membership of permanent and non-permanent members.

The General Assembly

The General Assembly (GA) is the main deliberative organ of the United Nations. It is composed of one representative from each member state, each of which has one vote. It is sort of like the UN's legislature where all the general debates are held. The significance of having all 193 member states debating together in one place for three months of the year (September to December)—and on 24-hour call the rest of the time—cannot be over-emphasized. Whether they like it or not, they are learning to apply the rules of international law, diplomacy and even democracy. They practice getting along and listening to one another. They learn to live by the rules of the game—and, indeed, determine what the rules of the game are. They learn to persuade rather than to fight. This is no small matter when you consider the UN has grown from 51 members when it was founded in 1945 to 193 members by 2011 (the year that the last new member, South Sudan, joined). Thus, the GA is a cornerstone institution which demonstrates the UN's distinctive universality—the very thing from which it derives its legitimacy. That may be why so many heads of state turn up for its annual general debate each September, which symbolizes the UN's convening power. Together, the above attributes define what is called the principle of 'multilateralism'. Nonetheless, we have to recognize that since the 1980s, the Assembly has been largely eclipsed by the more active Security Council and by the fact that major states have turned to institutions or grouping such as the World Bank and the Group of 20 to manage international economic relations.

Article 11 of the UN Charter authorizes the General Assembly to "consider" and "discuss" peace and security and "make recommendations" to members, except on issues being considered by the Security Council, to which it must also refer questions of "action". Article 13 spells out the GA's main fields of competence. It shall initiate studies and make recommendations for political cooperation, development of international law, and promoting international cooperation in the "economic, social, cultural, educational and health fields", as well as assist in the realization of "human rights and fundamental freedoms". Often fundamental developments can take a long time. For instance, the Maltese ambassador's well-known speech in 1967, which called for international regulations relating to the sea and proposing that the seabed and its resources were the "common heritage of mankind", was just the start of a 15-year long debate that eventually led to the Law of the Sea. Even so, we should note that it is often the bilateral and multilateral discussions that go on outside the formal debates that make the more significant contribution to the peaceful unfolding of world affairs.

The Assembly elects a new president each year as well as 21 vice-presidents and the heads of its six Main Committees. Anyone can become involved. Whether countries are small, medium or large, the Assembly tends to give as many delegates as possible some position of responsibility—with attendant recognition and rewards. Yet not all relations are cozy. Power has shifted in the Assembly since 1945 as the regional distribution of states has changed. From the UN's inception to the present day, the number of African states has increased from 3 to 54, those of Asia have risen from 9 to 53, while those of the West and Latin America have only doubled, from 39 to 85. The GA is riven by all sorts of groupings, mainly regional and the North–South split but also historical (the British Commonwealth) and cultural/linguistic (Spanish, French, Arab, etc.).

The two major blocs representing the 'developing countries' of the 'South' are the Non-Aligned Movement (NAM) with its 114 members and the Group of 77 with 133 members—many of them overlapping. The NAM was formed during the Cold War as a home for those who did not simply want to be swept up in the Communist-Capitalist divide. The G77 was founded several years later in 1964 to coordinate the position of developing countries on trade and development and to help them get a better collective grip on international trade and finance. Together they work to defend the General Assembly against what they perceive to be US dominance and attempts by the Great Powers to marginalize them. Some see the NAM as a holdover generally used to oppose the United States. Nonetheless, it is claimed that the Third World majority was hobbled by the fact that its majority inside the Assembly is not paralleled by resources for action outside. This highlights the GA's weakness as a deliberative body without effective administrative and coercive capabilities. This is in addition to the fact that the blocs tend to slow the process and bring decisions down to the 'lowest common denominator'—all of which underlies the tendency to want to boot all the action up to the Security Council.

The General Assembly's recommendations or "resolutions" are only binding when they apply to the UN's internal operations such as budget and membership matters. It elects the rotating members of the Security Council and the

Economic and Social Council, and, along with the Security Council, it elects the judges of the International Court of Justice. It appoints the secretary-general on the recommendation of the Security Council.

The Assembly's current agenda runs to some 175 items arrayed across nine broad categories. To get through the agenda, the GA relies on its committee system to examine issues and propose solutions. There is a General Committee, a Credentials Committee and six Main Committees (see Box 3).

Box 3: The General Assembly's six Main Committees

First Committee – Disarmament and National Security

Second Committee – Economic and Financial

Third Committee – Social, Humanitarian and Cultural

Fourth Committee – Special Political and Decolonization

Fifth Committee – Administrative and Budgetary

Sixth Committee – Legal

Although these committees handle discussion of the main issues before the UN, the actual agenda reflects the more day-to-day workings of the world such as sustained economic growth and sustainable development; drug control, crime prevention and combating terrorism; disarmament; and maintenance of international peace and security. As can be imagined, each of these items has many subsections.

One of the main functions of the General Assembly is as a repository for international treaty making. Much international, multilateral activity and international law is treaty based. Treaties are also called covenants. The United Nations itself is essentially a treaty among all its state members (through the Charter). A member state becomes 'party' to a treaty by formally 'consenting to be bound' by its terms, usually via 'ratification' of the treaty by its legislature. Each treaty sets out a minimum number of states that must ratify it for it to become international law by which its signatories are bound. Later, other states may accede to the treaty/convention. An oversight committee is often established as a 'convention secretariat' to monitor the implementation of the treaty.

The most significant criticism of the General Assembly is that it does not represent the world effectively. With the GA's 'one member, one vote' policy, China gets the same representation as Malta. In 2013, 39 member states had populations under one million and 13 had populations under 100,000. The 65 least populated member states could together block a two-thirds majority vote, despite comprising less than 1 per cent of the total population of all member nations. And, theoretically, the 128 least populated members—which account for less than 8.5 per cent of humanity and collectively pay under 1.3 per cent of the total UN budget—could provide the two-thirds majority required to adopt a resolution (Schwartzberg 2013: 19-20). In other words, the power in the General Assembly is skewed *away from* the largest states. As Schwartzberg concludes from these figures, "If one is to oppose—quite rightly—the undemocratic veto by any one of the five strong nations with permanent membership in the SC, one should also oppose unwarranted exercises of political power by GA coalitions of the very weak." (ibid: 20).

There are also criticisms of the GA's ineffectual processes. It is accused of debating minutiae and of being unable to reach closure on issues that squander its prestige. Past secretaries-general have noted its need to streamline procedures and structures. In fact, most of the largest countries have 'voted with their feet' and fled the UN to work through the more restrained membership of the G7 and the G20. To overcome these deficiencies there are proposals for 'weighted voting' that would combine a country's population and economic contributions with its vote as a state (see Schwartzberg 2013). It is certainly clear that reforms are needed to attract the important players to reconsider the United Nations as an effective forum of global decision-making.

The Economic and Social Council

ECOSOC is the acronym used to refer to the third principal organ of the UN, the Economic and Social Council. Its primary functions are to be a central forum for discussing economic, social and environmental issues, to formulate policy recommendations for states and the UN, and to integrate the three pillars of sustainable development. The UN Charter spells out both its policy and advocacy roles, stating that it may make or initiate studies with respect to international economic, social, cultural, educational, and health matters, as well as human rights; make policy recommendations to the General Assembly; and convene conferences. It is also responsible for coordinating the work of UN agencies (e.g., UNICEF, UNESCO) in these fields and is the intermediary between the GA and the more than 30,000 NGOs doing development work and humanitarian advocacy (including the approximately 4,000 that have consultative status with ECOSOC).

The Council's current 54 members, elected by the General Assembly on a geographical basis, serve three year terms. They elect their own president and four vice-presidents every year. Decisions are by majority vote with each member having one vote. It holds preparatory meetings along with relevant NGOs and then holds a four-week substantive session in July, alternating between New York and Geneva. This session includes a high-level segment that cabinet ministers and other officials are meant to attend. The Council is intended to coordinate the work of UN programmes and funds, and specialized agencies. The year-round work of ECOSOC is carried out by its subsidiary and related bodies including: eight functional commissions (statistics, population, social development, women, narcotics, crime, science and technology, and forests and sustainable development—now a high-level political forum); five regional commissions (Africa, Asia-Pacific, Europe, Latin America and Caribbean, and Western Asia); three standing administrative committees; a Permanent Forum on Indigenous Issues; and a number of expert bodies (for instance on tax matters and transport of dangerous goods).

ECOSOC has long been criticized for its ineffectiveness. There have been many efforts to reform it over the decades, and yet it is perhaps the organ that has shown the least amount of change. Its difficulties stem from a host of reasons. First, its responsibilities and functions often overlap with those of the General Assembly. Although the Charter elevates ECOSOC to the rank of a principal organ, it also clearly places it under the authority of the GA. As we saw above, the Second Committee of the GA deals with economic and financial matters, while the Third Committee's mandate covers the social, humanitarian and cultural fields. On top of this duplication, the Assembly has the advantage of being the UN's foremost plenary debating society where everyone has a voice, while ECOSOC is one-quarter its size.

Second, many large countries, particularly Western, industrialized nations, have long sought to limit the UN's voice when it comes to the international economy. They certainly do not want the UN to be the central forum for debating and coordinating economic policy. Nor do they want to be held hostage to listening to the grievances of the scores of small and poor developing countries that dominate the General Assembly and ECOSOC. This sheds light on why, at the creation of the UN, the Great Powers shovelled the serious economic matters to the independent World Bank and International Monetary Fund where they not only control the agenda but also nominate leaders. This was part of a long process of diverting the UN away from macro-economic policy-making and toward development assistance. More recently, the wealthiest countries have fled the UN in the direction of the G7 and the G20 to discuss economic matters.

Third, in order to promote decentralization, the founders of the UN endowed the 14 Specialized Agencies with their own governing apparatus. Each one reports to its own state authorities. The result is that they have never felt compelled to want to be 'coordinated' by ECOSOC. As if these fundamental problems were not enough, the very ponderous nature of ECOSOC also dooms it to irrelevance. Its 54 members are too numerous to be decisive and too few to have the attraction of the General Assembly. Its processes and meetings are too cumbersome to attract powerful ministers and to deal with emergency issues when the UN really needs to be active.

ECOSOC has been adorned with such adjectives as 'fuzzy', 'powerless' and 'lacking a clear identity'. Proposed reforms have run into the opposition of foreign ministries of powerful countries, the General Assembly or the Security Council. So, ECOSOC continues to limp along helping to advance programs for development and technical matters. It does now meet with the international financial institutions and interacts with the Security Council, but the issues of its ambiguous relations with the General Assembly, the non-binding nature of its decisions and its composition remain to be solved. Chapter 3 will explore some past attempts at reform, as well as ideas put forward by experts to transform ECOSOC into a workable institution.

Trusteeship Council

There is an additional, little known principal organ of the UN, now in disuse. It is the Trusteeship Council, originally created in 1945 to administer and supervise the 80 countries still under colonial jurisdiction while on their path to independence under the guidance of the UN. Palau, a small island group in the Pacific, was the last trust territory before becoming a UN member in 1994. Despite considerable thought and effort by Secretary-General Kofi Annan, a majority could never be rallied behind any of the propositions for an amendment to the Charter to change the Council's vocation (e.g., to be an environmental council). Hence, the Trusteeship Council simply suspended operations in 1994 and ceased to exist except on paper. This story demonstrates that the founders of the UN could not foresee every eventuality. It also illustrates how difficult it would be to amend the Charter, even when there is relative consensus on non-threatening modifications to better reflect the current reality. Despite the hurdles that would need to be overcome, the former Trusteeship Council is available to be used for some new purpose.

The International Court of Justice

The International Court of Justice (ICJ), founded in 1946 as part of the Charter, is the principal judicial organ of the United Nations. Located in The Hague (the Netherlands), it is the only one of the six principal organs not located in New York. Also known as the 'World Court', it is the only court of a universal character with general jurisdiction. Its first role is to settle legal disputes submitted by states in accordance with international law (see Box 4). There are more than 180,000 inter-state treaties in the UN registry and over 500 major multilateral treaties, for which the secretary-general is the repository. ICJ judgements have binding force for the parties concerned and are without appeal. Second, the Court gives advisory opinions on legal questions referred by UN organs and agencies.

Box 4: Understanding 'international law'

In general, international law includes duly ratified international treaties and conventions, decisions of the Security Council, international custom, the general principles of law, and, in a subsidiary manner, previous judicial decisions and the teachings of the most notable international law experts. In a broader sense, 'soft-law' may include declarations, statements, and plans of action agreed to by signatory countries or international conferences. Together they provide the norms of international law, but not the coordinating framework for an international legal regime.

The International Law Commission was established by the General Assembly in 1947 to promote the progressive development of international law and its codification. A major part of their work is preparing drafts of aspects of international law and submitting them to the GA. The GA may then convene a conference to incorporate the draft into a convention, open to states to become parties if they agree to be bound by its provisions. Some regulate relations between states such as the Conventions on Diplomatic Relations, Consular Relations and the Law of Treaties. There are also a number of extensive bodies of law such as International Trade Law and Environmental Law. One of the world's most comprehensive instruments is the United Nations Convention on the Law of the Sea, with its 320 articles and nine annexes. It is now universally accepted that all activities and resources in the oceans and seas are governed by the Convention, with its 165 states parties. For instance, there is general acceptance of 12 nautical miles as the limit of a country's territorial sea and also of an exclusive economic zone and also continental shelf zone up to 200 miles. The Convention has also brought stability to navigation, establishing the right of innocent passage in territorial waters, transit passage in narrow straits, and freedom of navigation in the exclusive economic zone.

The ICJ has delivered fewer than 100 judgements on cases running from boundaries and sovereignty to violations of humanitarian law and diplomatic disputes. It has also rendered 27 advisory opinions. Thus, the Court is not exactly over-worked. This is in part because only member states can submit disputes (no individual or other international actor can bring a case forward) and states must bind themselves in advance to accept the ruling. The ICJ is not a 'constitutional court' for the UN system and has no legal review of decisions. There is also little power of enforcement.

The International Court of Justice is now buttressed by the International Criminal Court (ICC), an independent permanent court founded by the Rome Statute in 1998 and entered into force in 2002. By 2013 it had been ratified by 122 states parties. It tries persons accused of 'international crimes': genocide, crimes against humanity and war crimes. We include it here for completeness; however, it is not part of the United Nations. Its creation was facilitated by the

UN and cooperation between the ICC and the UN is governed by a 'negotiated relationship agreement'. The Security Council can refer cases to it. The ICC is discussed in further detail in Chapter 4.

In its attempts to expand international humanitarian law, the Security Council also established the International Criminal Tribunals for the former Yugoslavia (1993) and for Rwanda (1994) and supported the special courts for Sierra Leone (2002), Cambodia (2006) and Lebanon (2007). These are sometimes referred to as 'hybrid courts', which cease to exist once all cases have been heard.

The Secretariat

The Secretariat includes all departments and offices that develop policy and administer the UN. It is the head and the heart of the international organization. Despite continuous accusations of a 'huge bureaucracy' from enemies of the UN, the reality is that there are only around 40,000 staff (as of June 2016), comparable to the personnel of some municipalities and indeed less than that of the New York City police and fire departments. Of these, roughly half are located in the field; the remaining half are based out of cities where the Secretariat has a presence, mainly New York where it is headquartered but also Geneva, Vienna, Nairobi and others. The Secretariat services the other principal organs and administers the programs and policies they establish. The duties carried out by the Secretariat include: peacekeeping administration, mediation of international disputes, organizing humanitarian programs, surveying economic and social trends, studies on human rights and sustainable development, and promoting international agreements. It also has the task of developing public information and organizing international conferences.

The list of departments and offices within the Secretariat (see Figure 2) shows the immense scope of UN activities. In addition to the diverse responsibilities listed above, it must also stay abreast of current affairs, whether related to economic and social affairs, peacekeeping or human rights. Given the 'globalization of everything', from financial instability to the movement of people, this is no easy task. To finance its work, the Secretariat's 2016-2017 budget was approximately $2.4 billion—about half the UN's total biennium budget for these two years. To secure the human and financial resources to carry out its responsibilities, the secretary-general and his assistants must continually bargain, negotiate and 'beg, borrow and steal' with the member states and, to a lesser extent, the corporate sector.

It can be said that over time the Secretariat has been as well run as any bureaucracy. In response to multiple criticisms (especially from the Americans), it has been studied, restructured and seen its budget and personnel reduced many times. For instance, in 1997-98 Kofi Annan brought together some thirty departments, funds and programmes into four executive groups for Development; Political and Security Affairs; Humanitarian Affairs; and Human Rights—a basic model which is still adhered to. New safeguards on spending and corruption are continually instituted.

The real problem with the Secretariat lies in the refusal of nation-states to allow it to be a fully meritocratic international public service as was originally tried with some success under the League of Nations. Everyone, the major powers included, has reasons for wanting to control the secretariat—or not wanting someone else to do so. In 1945 it was intended in Charter Articles 100 and 101 that staff members would be independent of any government. Article 100 enunciated the principle of an independent, international civil service and Article 101 spelled out the overriding values of the "highest standards of efficiency, competence and integrity". But under pressure from the Soviet Union, a 'gentleman's agreement' was reached in London in 1946 and the five permanent members were 'assigned' major departments of the Secretariat. This was the beginning of the seesaw battle that has continued ever since between those who want a professional and independent public service and those who want to place their nationals in strategic positions. The latter have been winning. Reinforced by demands for 'geographical distribution', there has been a growing politicization of the Secretariat over the years and often poor management, lack of accountability and cronyism. Staff members have also complained about poor administrative justice in the Secretariat (Jonah 2007: 165).

Beyond the organs

The Secretary-General

> *"There are limits to what the Secretary-General can do... Multilateral institutions (such as the UN) are conditioned by changing international power configurations, and by conflicts that exist within the broader international system"* Edward Newman (2007: 189)

Active and skilful secretaries-general such as Dag Hammarskjöld and Kofi Annan have managed to transform a rather benign position into a "symbol of the United Nation's ideals and a spokesperson for the interests of the world's peoples" (UN Information Service). The secretary-general is named by the General Assembly upon the recommendation of the Security Council for a term of five years. Almost all have completed two terms (see Box 5 for the complete list of past SGs). The description of the position in the Charter is very skimpy. It says little more than, "he shall be the chief administrative officer of the Organization" (UN Charter, Article 97). The UN's description of the position is a little clearer, stating that the secretary-general "establishes general policies and provides overall guidance to the organization and is in equal parts diplomat and advocate, civil servant and chief executive officer" (Basic Facts about the UN 2014: 17). Tradition has it that the founders expected the SG to be more secretary than general. Nevertheless, the world expects him to 'speak truth to power' by telling "the Security Council what it has to know, not what it wants to hear", as Michael Sheehan, former assistant secretary-general for peacekeeping, put it (Fasulo 2015: 27). In fact, the most significant function of the SG is to make the Council aware of any impending dangers to peace and security.

Box 5: Secretaries-General, 1945-present

Trygve Lie (Norway)	1946-1952
Dag Hammarskjöld (Sweden)	1953-1961
U Thant (Burma)	1961-1971
Kurt Waldheim (Austria)	1972-1981
Javier Pérez de Cuellar (Peru)	1982-1991
Boutros Boutros-Ghali (Egypt)	1992-1996
Kofi Annan (Ghana)	1997-2006
Ban Ki-moon (South Korea)	2007-2016
Antonio Guterres (Portugal)	2017-

The SG also chairs the Chief Executives Board of the UN system including all the funds, programmes and agencies, and the World Bank and the International Monetary Fund. This is as close as the UN gets to coordination. Traditionally the SGs have rotated among the world's regions. All have been men, but the calls for a woman head of the UN have become louder.

Needless to say, the secretary-general cannot do everything him or herself. The SG is surrounded by 15 under-secretaries-general who manage the various departments of the Secretariat. Since 1998, the SG has also been seconded by a deputy secretary-general to help with the administrative burden and special activities. To help carry out the secretary-general's all-important use of his 'good offices' (negotiation, mediation, conflict prevention, public relations, arm twisting in public and private, etc.), the SG can name special and personal representatives and envoys, including 'Messengers of Peace' and 'Goodwill Ambassadors'. Each secretary-general also must focus the UN's activities dependent on the international context. For example, Ban Ki-moon's focus for his second term from 2012 to 2016 included sustainable development, climate change, prevention of natural disasters, armed conflict, human rights abuses, a more secure world, nations in transition, and women and youth.

One analyst has summed up very well the complexities of the secretary-general's position. "Without the traditional levers of power, the Secretary-General can nevertheless wield real influence in international politics through the use of moral suasion and his authority as the embodiment of the 'international community'. However, this is always within the context of an organization controlled by member states which have as their primary concern their national interests." (Newman 2007: 175).

Given the significance of the secretary-general's position, there have always been debates over the scope of its powers and the mode of nomination. The nomination comes from the Security Council, which essentially means those states which can veto any proposal (the Permanent Five members, though in effect just the largest—the United States, China and Russia). There has been no openness, foresight or planning. Critics have long called for a serious selection process with specified qualifications, an extended search, rules for nomination, a timetable for discussion and a single seven-year term to avoid politicking. Thanks to the 1 for 7 Billion campaign led by the World Federalists Movement and the British United Nations Association, the Security Council finally relented in 2015 and gave the critics half a cake. It was decided that while the method of selection would go according to tradition, there would be an open nomination process for all countries and candidates would make their case to the General Assembly. There were 10 official candidates in the 2016 selection for the next secretary-general. Half the candidates were women, following significant pressure for a woman to hold the top post. The entire process was more transparent than it had been in the past, with public dialogue and televised debates. But the single nomination still came from the Security Council, and it was done in secret.

The candidate finally chosen by the Security Council and elected by the General Assembly was Antonio Guterres. Mr. Guterres served as Prime Minister of Portugal (1995-2002) and as the UN High Commissioner for Refugees for two mandates (2005-2015). He was known at the UN for maintaining good relations with member states, civil society and the private sector. He also reformed and innovated in his Office while minimizing its costs.

In his 'vision statement' presented to the General Assembly in April 2016, Antonio Guterres summarized his intended priorities for the coming years. He spoke to the need for new approaches to deal with the challenges of our time, which include inequality, exclusion and the changing nature of conflict. He envisioned a UN that is able to 'connect the dots' through a holistic approach that effectively links the three pillars of peace and security, sustainable development and human rights. To achieve this, Guterres highlighted the importance of reforming the UN Development System, mainstreaming both human rights and gender equality across the whole UN system, and implementing the Agenda 2030, the Paris Climate Agreement, and the Addis Ababa Action Agenda. He went on to emphasize the centrality of prevention in ensuring peace and security, and specifically the need for diplomacy, the participation of women and institution building. Reform and innovation, focused on delivery and results, is another key priority outlined. He stated his view that reform is not a onetime action but a permanent attitude, and that efforts should centre on being less bureaucratic and more productive, efficient and field oriented. Finally, he called for strong partnerships with regional organizations, the international financial institutions, civil society and the private sector.

UN budgets

The United Nations General Assembly approved a two-year UN budget of $5.4 billion for 2016-2017, down 1 per cent from the total spending during the previous two years. The new biennial budget includes a 2 per cent staffing cut, or some 221 posts, and a one-year freeze in staff compensation. This is not the first time there has been a decrease in the UN budget. In fact, the organization is almost always held on a short financial leash by member states. Many critics believe the endemic underfunding of the UN is its most crucial problem. On the other hand, many members, led by the United States, have over the years accused the Secretariat of being a bloated bureaucracy and profligate spender—whether this be a gross exaggeration or not.

As in past years, the biennial budget negotiations were marked by a tussle between poor countries seeking to increase the UN development spending, and major developed countries, the biggest budget contributors, trying to rein in the figures as they struggle to reduce expenditures in their own national budgets.

The so-called core UN budget that was adopted does not include peacekeeping, currently running at over $8 billion a year and approved in separate negotiations. Noteworthy is the fact that the total peacekeeping budget represents less than half of one per cent of annual world military spending, estimated at $1.7 trillion in 2016, or 2.3 per cent of world gross domestic product (GDP). Nor does the core budget cover the costs of the UN tribunals. Both the peacekeeping and the tribunals are covered by payments assessed by the Assembly, mainly among the wealthier countries. The individual budgets of the major UN agencies and programmes (such as UNICEF, UNHCR, UNDP, UNESCO and WHO) are funded by voluntary contributions from member states.

The UN System

Technically speaking, the 'United Nations System' is formed of the UN family of organizations that includes the principal organs, the United Nations programmes and funds, the specialized agencies and other related organizations (although many of us do use the term UN System more loosely to refer to all

Figure 2: The United Nations System diagram

Source: United Nations

organisms related to the UN). Programmes, funds and offices are subsidiary bodies of the General Assembly. On the other hand, the specialized agencies are independent but are linked to the UN through individual agreements and report to ECOSOC and/or the Assembly. There is also a difference in funding. While all subsist on chronically inadequate voluntary contributions from member countries, the specialized agencies also receive contributions from the overall UN budget. The International Atomic Energy Agency and the World Trade Organization are considered to be 'related organizations' with their own legislative bodies. As we just saw, an attempt to coordinate the UN system is made by the United Nations System Chief Executives Board for Coordination. With its 29 members and chaired by the Secretary-General, it meets twice a year.

The need for better coordination across the system has been an issue for decades. In fact, in their analysis of the lack of institutional coherence of the UN system, Childers and Urquhart concluded that the founders understood from the outset that a loose assemblage of agencies could not provide adequate governance. Recognizing this, the founders had specifically designed linkages that could make a loose collection of organizations work. From the outset it was intended that the UN would be the authoritative hub "able to forge coordinated strategies" (1994: 40), while the specialized agencies (by signed legal agreements under Articles 57, 58 and 63 of the Charter) were meant to have their objectives coordinated along with varying degrees of administrative harmonization and coherence. Yet these were never implemented. Moreover, while it was deliberate that specialized agencies would have their own separate legal existence and secretariats (so that politicians and diplomats could not hinder progress on specialized and technical matters), it was never envisaged that the agencies would grab the degree of separateness that has become one of the system's chief weaknesses.

As the authors deduce, "There is no intergovernmental assembly or council of the UN system as a whole." (ibid: 31). Now we see why so many 'reformers' are turning to a restructured ECOSOC as the potential new central pillar for economic, social and environmental policy cohesion.

International financial institutions and other international actors

The two major international financial institutions, the World Bank Group and the International Monetary Fund, are in a class apart. Founded at the Bretton Woods Conference in 1944, they are also known as the Bretton Woods institutions. Although they are completely independent, they are considered to be two of the 15 Specialized Agencies of the United Nations with which they maintain formal relations through the Chief Executives Board for Coordination. However, the founders of the UN specifically separated these two major financial institutions from the rest of the UN, presumably to reduce political interference and provide for shareholder governance as described below.

The World Bank Group evolved from the International Bank for Reconstruction and Development (that facilitated post-Second World War reconstruction) to today's five financial institutions with a mandate to provide financing and technical assistance for worldwide poverty alleviation. The five institutions are: the International Bank for Reconstruction and Development, the International Development Association, the International Finance Corporation, the Multilateral Investment Guarantee Agency and the International Centre for Settlement of Investment Disputes.

In 2016, the World Bank Group provided $64.2 billion for financial and technical assistance to developing countries around the world, making it one of the largest sources of such financing. This assistance supports a wide array of investments in such areas as education, health, public administration, infrastructure, financial and private sector development, agriculture, and environmental and natural resource management. The International Bank for Reconstruction and Development (IBRD) makes loans for development projects to governments of middle income and creditworthy low-income countries; in 2016 it made new commitments of $29.7 billion in 114 operations. The International Development Association (IDA) provides interest free loans (called credits) and grants to governments of the poorest countries with terms varying from 25 to 38 years. It made new commitments of $16.2 billion in 162 operations in 2016. Together, IBRD and IDA make up "the World Bank" (as opposed to "the World Bank Group" which consists of all five institutions).

The primary purpose of the International Monetary Fund (IMF) is to ensure the stability of the international monetary system—the system of exchange rates and international payments that enables countries to transact with each other. It does so in three ways: keeping track of the global economy and the economies of member countries; lending to countries with balance of payments difficulties; and giving practical help to members. For instance, along with European banks, it was the major lender to help Greece out of its troubles in 2014. The Fund's mandate was updated in 2012 to include all macroeconomic and financial sector issues that bear on global stability. Since the global economic crisis in 2009, it has also strengthened its support for low-income countries to respond to changing economic conditions and their increased vulnerabilities.

For both the Bank and the IMF, the 189 member countries subscribe funds according to their economic strength. Voting power is linked to the level of subscription. While the voting shares vary by organization, the US, Japan, Germany, France and Great Britain control roughly 35 per cent of the votes. Each member country appoints one governor and one alternate to the Boards of Governors, which meet annually. The governors are usually ministers of finance or governors of a central bank. Traditionally, the President of the World Bank has been American while the Managing Director of the IMF has been European.

However, the IMF has moved toward an open, merit based process for selection of the Managing Director in 2011 and the World Bank is likely to follow.

The international financial institutions do more than provide loans and regulate the international economy. They also impose conditions. Starting in the late 1980s, what was called the 'Washington Consensus' promoted neo-liberal rules to reduce the role of governments in the economy and increase the role of market forces. The World Bank and IMF were able to promote that view throughout the developing world by attaching policy conditions to the major loans they made for budgetary support. Countries were obliged to cut public spending, eliminate subsidies, and privatize state-owned industries. Later in the 1990s this was described under the banner of 'good governance' and included democratization and transparency. As time went on it was recognized that these policies often spawned more poverty in developing countries and more foreign ownership. Government fiscal restraint sometimes made national financial emergencies worse rather than better.

Founded in 1995, the World Trade Organization (WTO) is a successor to the post-war General Agreement on Tariffs and Trade (GATT). Over 50 years, the GATT successfully cut tariff protection by more than half among member states, but it had several perceived weaknesses. Formal disputes among members, for instance, relied on the consent of all parties, including the defendant, to proceed. Countries could simply block proceedings against themselves, though, interestingly, they rarely did. Yet the WTO is a comparatively far more legalistic institution. It also has a broader scope, encompassing issues such as health and safety measures, and intellectual property. Like the GATT, the WTO continues to operate by a consensus voting rule. Combined with its large membership, which counts 164 members as of 2016, this consensus rule has been faulted by many for the institution's current stalemate: its last negotiation round, the Doha Round, has been stalled for over a decade. Yet one aspect of the institution, its dispute settlement function, continues to thrive. Among international courts, it stands out by its large caseload, with over 500 disputes filed, its high level of compliance with its rulings, and the consistency of its jurisprudence. Insofar as countries continue to liberalize trade under the WTO's auspices, it is through the continuous clarification of their obligations that occurs with the settlement of formal disputes. Although it is not a formal part of the UN, the WTO maintains regular relations with parts of the UN system.

The rise of other international actors cannot be ignored (see Box 6). Enumerated her are those that are now generally accepted in the international relations literature but we must keep our eyes open for powerful new partners on the global stage.

Box 6: Other 'actors' enter the world stage

The term 'actors', as it is used here, refers to groups which have a significant enough influence on international politics that they must be taken into consideration both by other players and by analysts. Up until the 1980s and 90s it was generally agreed the only influential actors in international politics were nations states and their creatures like the United Nations and other international organizations. One of the major changes in international politics is the presence of new actors which cannot be ignored. These, in particular, include civil society, in the form of NGOs, and the private sector represented by multinational corporations—but also the media, religious groups, regional actors, and major cities.

Civil society, which is considered the "third sector" of society, distinct from government and business, comprises NGOs, social movements, religious institutions, academics, unions and all other non-state organizations and institutions that promote the interests of citizens. A recent count placed the number of NGOs at more than 50,000; most created since the 1980s and 90s. Some NGOs have more resources than even UN agencies. Civil society is most effective when its members come together in what are called 'campaign coalitions' to influence major international decisions, such as the creation of the International Criminal Court, the ban on landmines, and R2P. It derives its strength, in great part, from having come to represent democratic forces and because it can influence public opinion, the media and corporations at both national and international levels. It is also a source of international expertise.

Similarly, the corporate world has become increasingly influential in international politics, where it is now considered to be an important partner. The relationship reached new heights in 2000 when the UN created the Global Compact to encourage businesses to adopt sustainability principles and report on their implementation. Over 9,000 companies have since joined the initiative.

Another set of new actors, the G7 and G20 provide ideal settings for economic influence. The Group of 7, made up of the wealthiest and most powerful Western allies and Japan, wanted a space for policy making that could focus on the political issues of the moment. The Group of 20 is composed of the world's largest economies. Some consider it a necessary institution to deal with world financial crises and economic planning away from the discordant demands of the UN. Others see it as the antithesis of attempts to create universal diplomatic forums. Concentrating on short term issues determined by the most powerful, it is a throwback to the Concert of Europe with no agenda for development and no secretariat to carry out any long term purposes. An increasingly important actor on the international stage is also the World Economic Forum, meeting annually in Davos, Switzerland. It claims to be committed to improving the state of the world and engages the foremost political, business and other leaders of society to try to shape global, regional and industry agendas.

Chapter 2 – Peace and Security: Fixing the Security Council

"Peace cannot be kept by force. It can only be achieved by understanding" Albert Einstein

We already outlined the Council's mission and structures in the last chapter. Now our task is to understand what works and what does not in the Security Council. In the UN, it is rarely all or nothing. We have to avoid the temptation to exaggerate. The Security Council has made great strides since the 1990s. And yet there remain fundamental blockages to its goal of overseeing peace and security in the world.

Most of us would like to take a straightforward, rational approach to analyzing a subject like the Security Council. Unfortunately, it does not lend itself well to seeking consistent explanations. It is too fraught with complexity, contradictions and anomalies to present purely reasonable conclusions. For instance, according to the UN Charter, all members are meant to be equal but the Permanent Five veto-holding members are evidently more equal than the others. While the Security Council is meant to uphold *international* peace and security, most of its energy is spent on interventionist peace operations *within* war-torn countries. The UN is not meant to meddle in the sovereign affairs of independent countries and yet the Security Council regularly does so with impunity. Despite the Charter, the Council has moved partially from a Westphalian sovereignty perspective toward global community responsibility. Another obvious conundrum is that the Security Council is responsible for peace and security and yet not only does it allow the bloodiest conflicts to go on endlessly but it sometimes appears that some of its members aid and abet them. So when we analyze the Security Council we must be at pains to sort out the wheat from the chaff and to seek underlying causes and explanations wherever possible. We also must blend our focus on the Security Council with an attention to the broader world security perspective.

Finally, by way of introductory comment, it should be stated that the meaning of 'peace and security' has evolved over the decades. Originally, it simply meant the 'national security' of the nation-state. Later it came to mean the 'common security' of the international or global community, which is chiefly the responsibility of the United Nations. More recently, 'human security' has been added to focus on individuals—especially civilians in war-torn situations—and the responsibility of governments to them.

In another sense the term refers to a whole array of global challenges that lead to 'insecurity'. A first example would be terrorism, which seeks to spread fear and conflict. States have been unable to even agree on a definition of terrorism, as one person's terrorist can be another person's freedom fighter or even agent of a government. Then there are mass migrations which, as we have seen in Europe, can upset the balance of societies, create frictions, lead to political disputes and even threaten regional integration efforts. The effects of climate change, including rising water levels, extreme weather conditions and greater migration, will only intensify. Pandemics can send whole countries and regions into a tailspin and cause an international blame-game. Cyber attacks are a less deadly but nevertheless destructive form of warfare. Economic shocks spread from one country to another. International crime and mafias demand international solutions.

At a moral level, the Charter names other forms of security including freedom from hunger and the right to housing, employment and health. Just where in all this is the Security Council meant to intervene?

As we have seen, there are jurisdictional disputes between the Security Council and the General Assembly. They first surfaced in 1950 with the Uniting for Peace Resolution 377 under Articles 10 and 11. In the Soviet Union's absence from the Security Council (which it was temporarily boycotting), the West did an end-run around the Council. Using the General Assembly's power to act for peace and security when the Security Council is incapable of doing so, it created a UN force under American leadership to halt the invasion of the south by North Korea.

Today there is another jurisdictional, North-South confrontation over the extension of the Council's mandate. When the Council thinks it should act, it does. It often does as it pleases because it is thought by some that its relatively restricted format provides the ideal setting to address world crises, whether they relate to peace and security or not. For instance, the Council formally addressed the HIV/AIDS issue in 2000 under the heading of 'vital security interests'. Later, in 2007, the United Kingdom called on the Council to debate the relationships between energy, climate and security. The Council has also paid considerable attention to the issues of violence against women and women's contributions to peace. So now the shoe is on the other foot and many GA members think the Council should stick to armed conflicts.

Having noted this jurisdictional dispute between the Assembly and the Council, let us now return to our more specific focus on how well the Security Council handles its central objective of dealing with peace, conflict and security, before going on to look more specifically at its expanded use of peace operations.

The Security Council's functions and activities

Security Council strengths

It has been said that there has not been a single day since the Second World War when there has not been deadly political conflict somewhere in the world. Often this calls for action by the United Nations. In response, the Security Council has accelerated its pace over the years; it adopted 685 resolutions during its first 46 years, then 1,650 in the following 26 years (1991-2016). No matter whether it is admired or not, it has become generally accepted that the Security Council must authorize the use of international force—exactly as the Charter says it should. In other words, one source of the Security Council's authority is the international law arising from the stipulation in the United Nations Charter that the use of force by one state against another is limited to situations of self-defence (Art. 51) or circumstances where force is authorized by the Security Council (Chapter VII). Thus, contrary to popular belief, there is no independent justification for "humanitarian intervention" or "responsibility to protect", both of which are subject to authorization by the Security Council. Of course, a state or a group of states may still take independent actions on the basis of a purported moral or political legitimacy, but they are not considered legal. In the rare exceptions where UN authority was not obtained, things generally have not ended well (for instance, the NATO 'humanitarian' intervention in Kosovo in 1999 and the U.S. led invasion of Iraq in 2003). Indeed, this aspect of international law has done much to protect the world since 1945, ensuring that armed conflicts between states remain uncommon.

More broadly, as the President of the General Assembly, Mogens Lykketoft, pointed out at the May 2016 High Level Thematic Debate on Peace and Security, the UN has helped restrain the world's largest powers, mobilized personnel and money for peacekeeping, established a clear legal framework on war and human rights, and helped reduce the threat of the world's most deadly weapons.

So, in effect, the Security Council has become a sort of executive body for dealing with world crises. And when the Council acts in harmony it has proven quite effective. For instance, in 2014 it unanimously agreed to place sanctions on six leaders of the Islamic State and Al Nusra in the heat of the Middle East crisis. It has also virtually eradicated the notion of absolute national sovereignty. Now states can no longer act with impunity with regard to their own population and the Council can interfere in state conflicts that can be said to threaten international security. As David Malone states in his essay on the Security Council, "The Council's decisions in the post-Cold War era have proved immensely influential, indeed transformative, on a normative level. By asserting the UN's responsibility to intervene, even in internal conflicts—where human rights and the humanitarian interests of populations are severely affected—Council decisions, arising from evolving interpretations of the Charter, have deeply affected the meaning of sovereignty." (2007: 133).

Over the years, the Council has expanded its search for peace, making use of the secretary-general's 'good offices' and engaging in fact-finding missions. It also uses 'Groups of Friends', that is to say countries which can be influential and can advise and help intervene in particularly thorny cases when the Council members, themselves, may not have sufficient contacts. As we explore later in this chapter, the UN has moved beyond peacekeeping to undertake military missions of peace-enforcement as it tackles more numerous and diverse conflicts such as protecting East Timor in 1999, turning back the Iraqi invasion of Kuwait in 1990, and intervening in the civil wars in Guatemala and El Salvador. The SC also empowers regional organizations and 'coalitions of the willing' to act on its behalf. In recent years, the African Union and the Economic Community of West Africa (ECOWAS) have played leading roles in trying to tame conflicts in Darfur, Sierra Leone, Liberia and Côte d'Ivoire.

Sometimes the Security Council acts as one. Sometimes it is just the permanent members calling the shots. Sometimes it is just the United States, Russia or China individually pushing their weight around. Other times there are temporary alliances among some of the 15 members. However, aside from straight power and national interests, the Council can also be seen from the perspective of leadership. Getting things done among the 193 members of the UN often takes leadership and determination, as well as long term planning and diplomacy. The United States is often accused of calling the shots but usually its role comes down to drafting resolutions, getting votes and putting things together—in other words, providing leadership. The Council's difficulty in dealing with terrorism is a good example. Although it has adopted many strong, action-oriented resolutions to control terrorism, it is still not able to develop a consensual definition of the meaning of terrorism. Despite this, the leadership of a few led to a heads-of-state summit condemning terrorism in 1992, the pursuit of the Taliban in Afghanistan after 9/11, and sweeping decisions to combat terrorism financing and safe-havens and to create the Counter Terrorism Committee as a subsidiary body of the SC.

The Security Council is relatively more open, active and effective than we give it credit for. It now meets with states contributing to peace missions, NGOs, the business community, and regional organizations. Since the mid-1990s, the Council's president has been briefed informally by individual experts, NGOs and observers on special issues. There have been consultations with troop-contributing countries since 1994.

Given that the media often focuses on the inability of the UN to act in crises, it is rather astounding to learn that most Security Council resolutions are adopted. For instance, in 2016, there were some 457 meetings resulting in 72 resolutions which were adopted and only three vetoed. The percentage of vetoes as a portion of the total number of resolutions of the Council dropped from

85 per cent during the Cold War to 15 per cent after 1988. In other words, the major business of the Security Council goes on rather smoothly. Nevertheless, what the Council is known for is the relatively small number of resolutions that are vetoed by one or several of the Permanent Members (P5). From 2012 to 2017, Russia and usually China have vetoed resolutions on the Syrian civil war, impeding all consequential actions except for a small amount of humanitarian aid. One P5 veto, or the threat thereof, is sufficient to stop the Security Council, and hence the UN, from acting. This is even more significant now that, as we have just seen, the Security Council has spread its wings to consider ever more issues such as pandemics, climate change, health and economics.

As we have seen earlier, another facet of the Council's ability to influence the international system is through the use of mandatory sanctions to cut off a state's access to diplomatic relations, finance, trade and arms. Traditional sanctions, which were fairly broad in nature, have been criticized for causing more harm to the population at large than to the economic and/or political elites. Recent sanctions have been more focused, targeted at the travel, banking assets and luxury items of elites so as to have minimal effect on ordinary citizens. It has also become increasingly recognized that the main use of sanctions should be for persuasion rather than punishment. All in all, they have been used with considerable success against the apartheid regime of South Africa and the nuclear ambitions of Iran, but, so far, seem to have had little effect on the behaviour of North Korea. In the last decade, the public 'naming and shaming' of 'sanction busters' has added to the effectiveness of sanctions.

The Security Council has many other tasks as well. It nominates the judges of the International Court of Justice, with which it gets along well. The same cannot be said of relations with the International Criminal Court that was founded outside the UN and which the United States and China (as well as India, Israel and others) have refused to join. Though it is worth mentioning that the SC set up, on its own, ad hoc criminal tribunals for the former Yugoslavia in 1993 and Rwanda in 1994 as well as special courts for Sierra Leone in 2002 and for Cambodia in 2005. The Council is active in sending monitors to national elections when legitimized outcomes are crucial for developing democracy. It has 40 subsidiary bodies dealing mainly with fact-finding missions and implementation of sanctions but also with such continuing problems as counter-terrorism and children in armed conflict.

In sum, we may say that the UN Security Council since the 1990s has become far more open and partner-oriented and has developed a much larger and more diversified tool kit of means of intervention in peace and security. The cumulative effect has been an impressive list of achievements related to the UN's first pillar, peace and security (see Box 7).

Box 7: The UN's record of achievement in peace and security

- Helping avoid another global war.
- Amassing a body of international law, rules and legal norms including 560 international treaties since 1945, with their resultant normative impacts.
- Putting in place a system of dispute-settlement mechanisms including the International Court of Justice, the 1982 Law of the Sea, the 2005 Resolution of the Pacific Settlement of Disputes and the Mediation Support Office.
- Developing a network of 14 multilateral agencies to regulate international daily, vital, practical interaction—everything from telecommunications to tourism.
- Managing the proliferation of weapons of mass destruction and their inspection.
- Imposing sanctions on wayward state behaviour on 26 occasions.
- Deploying 54 peace operations and 39 special political missions designed to prevent, ameliorate or conclude conflicts.

Source: Rudd 2016: 11-16

Security Council weaknesses

Despite these achievements, all is not well with the Security Council. In its decisions, national self-interests too often clash with global security concerns. The great hopes people had for the Council as the peace-maker after the Second World War and after the Cold War were barely fulfilled. It did not translate itself into a collective body that was able to engage in the world's hot spots. There has been insufficient common leadership which has resulted in doubtful institutional legitimacy and international disenchantment. The contentious relations with the Non-Aligned Movement and the Group of 77 in the General Assembly only served to deepen the frustrations. The agreement of the P5 to help create the G20, comprising the world's most financially powerful nations, has further undermined the economic credibility of the United Nations. The Council is noted for being a reactive rather than a preventive body. The failure to include a set of operational criteria for activating the R2P norm symbolized this weakness perfectly. The Great Powers have not seen fit to equip the United Nations with its own emergency peace forces or autonomous finances, thus ensuring that the UN is kept on a leash.

Three failures of particular concern deal with nuclear weapons, global decision-making and a perception of growing irrelevance of the UN. The first UN resolution in January 1946 called for the elimination of weapons of mass destruction. But old-fashioned power politics took over from the hopes for collective morality. Principles gave way to national interests. The world descended into the Cold War dominated by the strategy of Mutual Assured Destruction. Although no nuclear arms have been used since Hiroshima and Nagasaki at the end of the Second World War, proliferation of nuclear arms and their delivery systems has gone on a pace. Initially limited to the US, France, Great Britain and the Soviet Union (now Russia), the number of nuclear armed states grew to include India, Pakistan, China and North Korea. Many believe Israel possesses nuclear weapons (though it has never admitted to it) and Iran sought to be included on the list.

Cognizant of the perils, a Non-Proliferation Treaty was established in 1968. Efforts were made in the 1972 SALT 1 treaty to cap the number of offensive nuclear weapons, but the 1980s saw a renewal of the arms race. Finally, the Comprehensive Test Ban Treaty was adopted in 1996. The underlying idea had been that nuclear states would agree to share peaceful nuclear technology with states that renounced efforts to have their own nuclear weapons, but there is dispute over whether the transfer has actually happened. Aside from these treaties was the creation of the International Atomic Energy Agency in Vienna in 1957. As an independent agency, it reports to the GA and SC on its mandate for control, verification, security, and technology transfer. Whenever it has been supported by the Security Council, it has done laudable work. But by the end of 2016, Trump and Putin were still talking about spending billions on modernizing their nuclear arsenals rather than technology transfer or ending poverty. Despite this, in 2017 a majority of 122 countries in the General Assembly voted for a treaty to ban nuclear weapons. All of the nine countries known or believed to have nuclear weapons boycotted the discussions claiming they disregard the "realities" of international security. The treaty will be open for signatures in late 2017 and will come into force when 50 countries have ratified it.

The second failure has been the inability of the Security Council to make decisions at crucial times at which the fate of whole peoples was under threat. The Council has not been able or willing to stop the most horrendous bloodbaths of our era is such cases as Bosnia, Rwanda, Zimbabwe, Darfur and Syria. In part, this has been because of the P5 veto or the threat of its use. This is paradoxical. The veto was the instrument invented to keep the major powers in the UN. In the modern era, great powers have never felt they had to threaten to quit the UN to defend their interests. But now they do not want to lose the power advantage the UN gives them.

Vetoes are a major cause of indecision in the Security Council, even if they have been declining in number. Vetoes are often not used to protect vital interests (e.g., to protect the state's national territory), but rather to maintain presumed spheres of influence and to protect allies as the US has done for Israel and Russia for Syria. They are also thought to heighten international status and strengthen public opinion at home. In other words, the P5 find plenty of reasons other than their vital interests for using the veto. Thus even without the veto we would still have big power politics in the Security Council and a disruption of global decision-making. That is why France and Mexico are pushing for a limit of the veto (which is possible) rather than its abolition (which is much less likely to happen).

Box 8: The Security Council's challenges, problems and failures

- Perceptions of impasse in the Security Council due to the veto and the threat of a veto feed frustrations about the UN's capacity to act to deal with crises, despite there being only 276 vetoes while 2,296 resolutions have been successfully adopted.
- Failure to prevent mass atrocities (war crimes, genocide, crimes against humanity) when the UN was slow or failed to respond—e.g., Cambodia, former Yugoslavia, Rwanda, Darfur, South Sudan, and Syria.
- Limited response to global terrorism including state-sponsored terrorism.
- Continuing repercussions from the invasion of Iraq against the UN's wishes.
- Absence of the UN from negotiations on the Iranian nuclear agreement and being used as an afterthought in Afghanistan.
- Lack of effective action to resolve the Syrian crisis, standing by as 400,000 have been violently killed and half the population uprooted.
- Lack of involvement in the Ukraine crisis.
- No UN diplomatic initiative against North Korea's illegal nuclear program.
- Inability to handle the 2015-16 wave of refugees, migrants and asylum-seekers.
- Loss of moral authority due to inconsistent response to human rights violations.
- Sexual abuse in peacekeeping operations tarnishes reputation of blue helmets.
- UN forces responsible for cholera outbreak in Haiti that killed thousands.

Source: Rudd 2016: 16-20

While these (along with the other failures listed in Box 8) can be considered legitimate limitations or flaws of the Security Council, the last issue relates more to how it is perceived. The word 'irrelevant' was first used by President George W. Bush in talking about the UN in 2003, and has become a refrain used by many others since. Of course, we have seen from the achievements of the Security Council that the UN is not in fact irrelevant. The world would be lost without all its contributions. Nevertheless, as regards perceptions, and oftentimes media coverage, it is another story.

We saw this in 2016 when, after the vetoing of another resolution on Syria in the Security Council, Canada was joined by 71 other countries in side-stepping the Council and bringing the issue directly to the floor of the General Assembly, in the manner of the 1950 Uniting for Peace resolution. This unique and newsworthy endeavour was barely mentioned by major newspapers. However, the next day, the nomination by the UN of Wonder Woman as an honorary ambassador was ridiculed in world headlines. It looks like irrelevance—or worse. Unfortunately, the tendency is still for the media to focus on the UN's shortcomings.

However, the consequences reach beyond simply harming public opinion of the UN. When the organization is regarded as being incapable of dealing with the most pressing security concerns, states have and will bypass it, as we saw when the Iran nuclear deal was negotiated in 2015.

The UN's peace operations

Historically, analysts have offered many different and sometimes conflicting explanations for the causes of war and the means of fostering peace. In *Man, the State, and War,* Kenneth Waltz (1954) was able to order these different approaches to causality under three headings: the individual, the state and the international system. Each one corresponds to a further analysis of what the type of causality portends for possible paths to peace. In the first, it is the bestial, aggressive nature of mankind which is targeted as the culprit. But, it is asked, if individuals are the cause of war, is it not the public institutions of the states which shape and limit their citizens? Then, it is further proposed that states too have to vie for themselves within the competitive, anarchical international system, leaving individuals and even states few choices in their behaviour. Waltz concludes that even these very general fields of causality may be further confused by the possibility that the causes of war may come from all three domains and even depend on particular circumstances.

Whatever the causes of war, the UN has been active in promoting peace since its inception. Before examining the evolution of UN peace operations, it is worth outlining some key terms related to the full scope of activities undertaken by the UN to maintain peace and security. These are: peacekeeping, peacemaking, peace enforcement and peacebuilding. Secretary-General Boutros Boutros-Ghali delineated these four distinctive but overlapping roles for peace operations in his 1992 Agenda for Peace. Peacekeeping, which broadly involves helping war-torn countries create conditions for lasting peace, is sometimes used in an all-encompassing sense to refer to other activities as well. Peacemaking (under Chapter VI of the Charter) refers to diplomatic action to bring hostile parties to an agreement, including through negotiation, enquiry, mediation, conciliation, arbitration, judicial settlement or with the help of regional agencies. The new methods that have been added to this long list have been the 'good offices' of the Secretary-General and his use of special envoys and representatives as mediators. Peace enforcement (under Chapter VII) requires the authorization of the Security Council and involves a range of coercive measures, including the use of military force. Finally, peacebuilding focuses on post-conflict recovery and reconstruction, aiming to build national capacities for conflict management and create the conditions for sustainable peace.

Although the first United Nations Emergency Force was deployed for the Suez crisis of 1956, the UN had already gained experience from monitoring and supervision operations as early as the 1940s. The original peacekeeping missions were limited to lightly armed forces acting as mediators and monitors, interceding between conflicting combatants to keep them apart—literally, to 'keep the peace'. They depended on the principles of consent, neutrality and the non-use of force.

Over the years, peace operations have expanded greatly in mission and mandate, going well beyond pure peacemaking, by working toward peacebuilding with the monitoring of elections and long-term international support for the development of institutions and finances in failed states. They may be authorized to use force and have police forces and administrative specialists overseeing the rebuilding of a functioning government and (hopefully) independent civil society. Operations have become multidimensional, aiming to facilitate the political process, protect civilians, promote human rights, support election, restore the rule of law, and assist in the disarmament, demobilization and reintegration of former combatants. As it may be imagined, such operations are frightfully complex.

What had changed was that from 1900 to 1941, 80 per cent of wars were between states; from 1945 to 1976, 85 per cent of wars were within a single state. These civil conflicts tended to be more all-encompassing and destructive of the economy, civil rights and state institutions. Many became mixed up in illicit trade and terrorism and conflicts threatened to spill over into neighbouring countries, thus endangering international peace. The UN was drawn in more and more. For the first time, operations came to combine both war-like enforcement and peace-like negotiations. In the post-Cold War period after 1990, the P5 in the Security Council were more cooperative and willing to tackle more numerous and diverse conflicts including domestic rivalries.

By 2016, there were 16 UN-led missions in the field for an annual cost of some $8.2 billion. They include large numbers of civilian and police components. The Department of Peacekeeping Operations in the Secretariat supervises more troops in the field—some 120,000—(contributed by members) than any individual country. There is often a need to work cooperatively with regional partners in 'coalitions of the willing' from groups such as NATO, the European Union, West African States and the African Union.

Over time, peacekeeping missions have been at once some of the UN's greatest successes and greatest failures. Among the successes were: the independence of Namibia; ending the conflict in El Salvador; demobilization, peace and reestablishment of Cambodia; peace, disarmament and elections in Mozambique; independence and a new government in East Timor; and ending the civil war and re-establishing the government in Sierra Leone. Terrible failures were in Somalia, Bosnia, Rwanda and Syria, where the Security Council refused to mobilize sufficient forces to control the situation and civilians were slaughtered by the thousands.

A great deal of research has been done to better understand why some missions succeed while other fail. Doyle and Sambanis found that the success of peace settlements depends on three factors: the degree of hostility, local capacities left over after the conflict, and the amount of international assistance available. Optimal intervention strategies need to match means to ends. Consideration has to be given to local causes, levels of conflict and hostility and factional capacities. A strategy of discrete acts of enforcement must be calculated to fit in with peacemaking (negotiations), peacekeeping (monitoring), and peacebuilding (reconciliation, reconstruction). This juggling act must be constituted within the context of military resources and civilian means for the rebuilding of institutions (2007: 323-348).

The UN itself has also initiated efforts to review its peace and security activities and recommend improvements. A particularly noteworthy study was the *Report of the Panel on United Nations Peace Operations,* commonly called the *Brahimi Report,* prepared in 2000 in response to significant UN peacekeeping failures in the 1990s. It called for "robust doctrines" and "realistic mandates" (referring to an explicit mandate for civilian protection and the resources to carry it out), improved headquarters management, and rapid deployment. The Security Council and the secretary-general delivered on all but the last, and many analysts agree that progress made in peacekeeping efforts was indeed influenced by the report.

Still, as the 2015 report of the High-Level Independent Panel on Peace Operations makes clear, there continues to be room for improvement. The report proposes a long list of operations improvements, such as clearer strategic direction, improved speed, strengthened partnerships, more purposeful engagement with host countries, and addressing sexual abuse which has tarnished the reputation of UN peacekeeping in recent years. The report also recognizes that certain political realities limit the UN's ability to consolidate peace. These include the fact that neither governments nor regional groupings fully entrust the UN with preventive diplomacy, and that the UN continues to be a relatively minor player in the field of international cooperation. This recognition is important when thinking about the future of the UN because it highlights a situation that is the inverse of what it should be if we want to enhance peace and cooperation. State diplomacy, focused on maximizing national interests, is currently winning over global diplomacy—this must change if we are to achieve a renaissance of the United Nations.

As this section has shown, the UN has an elaborate structure of prevention and peace operations. However, a number of tendencies have limited success. First, powerful states have sought to avoid assertive secretaries-general therefore limiting the role SGs can play in international diplomacy. Second, the UN's ability to prevent conflicts depends on the political will of member states. Unfortunately, the Security Council is oriented toward "the visible, forceful and reactive rather than the invisible, quiet and proactive initiatives required for dispute settlement" (Mani 2007: 318). This relates to perhaps the main challenge with prevention: successful instances are all but invisible, and the more effective it is, the less likely it is to make headlines. A final point is that global trends such as rising economic inequality, political marginalization and democracy movements tend to stimulate conflict, making prevention an onerous task.

The Security Council and the future

Reforming the Security Council is at once very simple and incredibly complex. There are many good ideas about what to do, but there are so many actors in the pot with too little common political will that nothing gets done. It is said that the Security Council is one of the major world arenas of power and realpolitik. Participation provides access, knowledge, power and influence. No wonder there is little consensus on who the players should be and what procedures are best. For us to see a little more clearly, we have to start with some basic principles and a set of objectives before going on to look at various reform proposals.

The basic principles that we should strive for are legitimacy and effectiveness. It is said that the power of social institutions resides mainly in their legitimacy. Writing about the legitimacy of the Security Council some years ago, David Caron stated, "For an institution to be considered legitimate it must be recognized as a lawful authority; one that conforms to a particular standard and operates in such a manner that its actions and decisions are seen as legally or morally justified and proper." (1993, 552). The United Nations is founded on an international treaty that all members have signed, so with this founding authority the Security Council may be said to be clearly lawful. As we have seen, its much improved manner of operation has made it more transparent and inclusive. Yet the organization is much larger now than in 1945, so the Council is no longer representative of the current UN membership. Also, because of its two-tier membership resulting from the veto, as well as the poor record of decision-making, it is no longer considered by many to uphold standards that are morally justified and proper. The second principle is effectiveness. Many question whether the Security Council is properly managing the world's peace and security and whether it is doing so in a manner that protects human rights and sustainable development. One also wonders just how big a Council could be to operate effectively and make decisions.

In terms of potential goals for a reform process, UN expert Andy Knight provides useful ideas: "improve the rate of participation from poorly represented categories; improve the geographical representation; improve its democratic character by limiting the use of the veto to Chapter VII actions and ensuring the Council represents a clear majority of the world's population; maintain its efficiency by limiting its growth; improve transparency by consulting with non-members on actions concerning them, and greater involvement of rotating members." (2002, 33-4). Thus, we have a set of objectives that cover diverse issues of size, fair representation, composition, legitimacy, efficiency and the veto.

The search for Security Council reform did not start yesterday. Resentment of the P5 members pushed the General Assembly to launch consultations on a reform agenda in 1993. It was called the "Open-ended Working Group on Equitable Representation". Two decades later it came to be known in the corridors of the UN as the 'Never-Ending Working Group'.

In a 2004 meeting in Baden-Baden, Austria, the secretary-general's High-Level Panel on Threats, Challenges and Change thought they had found the ideal solution on composition. The Council would be increased to 24 members in three tiers: tier one would include the present P5 (the US, Russia, China, Great Britain and France); tier two would include seven or eight semi-permanent members elected on a regional basis for a renewable term of four or five years (Brazil, Germany, India, Japan and South Africa might be in this group); the third tier of rotating members would be elected as at present for a non-renewable two year term. Only the Permanent Five would have a veto. More emphasis would be accorded to giving membership to those who make a real contribution to peace and security. A full review would be made every 15 years. The consensus in the Panel dissolved over a demand by some that all new tier two members be given a veto. The proposal never even got into the final report which included two inferior models catering to special interests. The secretary-general in effect threw up his hands and said members should vote for whatever they liked.

This example is given at length because it introduces most of the issues about composition and veto. As regards size, it is generally agreed that the 15-member Security Council should be expanded to be more representative of the world. The question is: by how much? More big powers may just add to the current conflict of interests and national prestige, making for more difficult decisions rather than easier. Still, most proposals come in the range of 20 to

25—small enough for discussion, big enough to be representative. All suggestions propose one to three more non-permanent, rotating seats. At present, the 10 rotating seats are for two-year terms elected by the General Assembly with three going to Africa, two to Western Europe and Oceania, two to Latin America and the Caribbean, two to Asia and one to Eastern Europe. Five are replaced each year and the elections are hotly contested.

Then we come to the crunch. Who should the new semi-permanent (or permanent) members of the Security Council be and should they have a veto or not? Surely countries as big as India, Japan, Brazil, South Africa, Indonesia, Nigeria, Germany and Pakistan should not be excluded from being Permanent Members? Alas, it is not so simple. Each of these countries has neighbours who are absolutely set against their elevation to a Permanent Member status.

At the 2005 World Summit, Japan, Germany, India and Brazil grouped together to form the G4. They were determined to get permanent seats but appeared willing to compromise on the veto. They had considerable support, but their regional rivals, including South Korea, Italy, Pakistan, and Argentina, immediately banded together with other countries like Canada, Mexico, Turkey and Spain in the 'Uniting for Consensus' group to propose there should be 10 new, non-permanent members with possibility for re-election, but no new permanent members. We see here one of the sticking points. Instead of acting like cozy regional friends, most neighbours are age old traditional enemies who do not want to see each other moving ahead. For their part, the African states proposed increasing the Council's membership from 15 for 26, introducing six new permanent seats with vetoes and five new rotating seats (granting Africa two seats in each category). At the present time the P5 represents four continents but not Africa.

When all is said and done, even if one were to find a workable model, nothing is to say that the current P5 would agree and not use their veto. Also, all these alliances are now a decade old and may have given way to other intentions. Nevertheless, they demonstrate to us the complexity of Security Council reform.

However, ten years does make a difference. In its 2015 report, the Commission on Global Security, Justice and Governance took a refreshingly different approach to reforming the UN Security Council. Showing that the world had moved on, instead of dwelling on the Council's composition, the Commission simply states that we must expand its membership and allow immediate reelection of non-permanent members in order to achieve the twin goals of effectiveness and acceptability.

When we think about transforming the Security Council, we should remember that if we are to make decisions for the good of the world, we will need something that looks like an 'executive committee' or a 'cabinet'. Perhaps all our present models are too wedded to the present context of 'nation-state international relations'. For 'global governance', we may need another model based on more state-like institutions with political and democratic foundations. In any case, we can imagine that it is going to take a lot of consultative thinking and perhaps a global movement to break all the impasses we have just seen and to press forward with all the potential reforms. We will return to these possibilities in Chapter 5.

"The future depends on what we do in the present." Mahatma Gandhi

Chapter 3 – Social and Economic Development

Understanding 'development'

The global understanding of development has changed over the years, as have definitions. Countries now agree that the best path forward is one of sustainable development, which the UN defines as "development that promotes prosperity and economic opportunity, greater social well-being, and protection of the environment". Sustainable development seeks to achieve these three pillars—economic development, social development and environmental protection—in a balanced manner. The term was originally coined in 1987 by the World Commission on Environment and Development in Our Common Future, in what became known as the *Brundtland report.* The report defines sustainable development as "development that meets the needs of the present without compromising the ability of future generations to meet their own needs". Thirty years later, this continues to be the most widely used definition.

Much of what the UN does falls into the broad category of 'development'. This includes work related to poverty reduction, food security, climate change, gender equality, housing, education, employment, infrastructure, disaster risk reduction, health and emergency response, water and sanitation, safety and crime prevention, good governance, and early childhood development. Even the areas of human rights and peace and security (the other two pillars of the UN's work) are now recognized as having important impacts on social and economic development. Their inclusion in the global post-2015 development agenda (Sustainable Development Goals) reflects these linkages.

This chapter explores what development meant at the UN's inception, the period of decolonization, and the introduction of the world's first global development agenda to mark the new millennium, as well as what it means in the present era of a second set of global goals. It looks at what lies ahead for the UN and assesses how prepared it really is to achieve the challenging task at hand.

The first 50 years

Development in the early years

Development is among the three founding pillars of the UN system. The UN Charter states that "the United Nations shall promote higher standards of living, full employment, and conditions of economic and social progress and development". Yet the understanding of development when the Charter was drafted was unique to that specific moment in history, and the concept evolved greatly over the years. Consider how the world looked in 1945. The original membership of the UN was 51 countries, of which the vast majority were European, Latin American, North American and the Middle Eastern states. The notions of developed and developing countries, North and South, First World and Third World simply did not exist at that time. Early development efforts of the international system focused on post-World War II reconstruction. In 1948, the US launched the Marshall Plan, a massive aid initiative to rebuild Western Europe following the devastation of the war. Through the Plan, officially known as the European Recovery Program, the US, aided by companion programs in Canada and other countries, channeled more than $12 billion over three years to finance the economic recovery of Europe—a region that, relatively speaking, was industrialized and economically advanced. Europe's swift recovery meant that the international community could soon focus its efforts elsewhere.

In the years that followed, the emphasis quickly shifted to developing countries that were gaining independence from their colonial powers. Between 1956 and 1968, UN membership grew from 80 to 126. Nearly all of these additional members were African and Asian countries, newly independent from European colonial powers. This period of rapid decolonization, which began in the late 1940s but accelerated in the two decades that followed, was prompted by the recognition that all peoples had the right to self-determination. In 1960, this basic right was formalized when the UN General Assembly adopted the Declaration on the Granting of Independence to Colonial Countries and Peoples, stating that "the subjection of peoples to alien subjugation, domination and exploitation constitutes a denial of fundamental human rights, is contrary to the Charter of the United Nations and is an impediment to the promotion of world peace and cooperation." It called for immediate steps to be taken in territories that had not yet attained independence to transfer power to the people to enable them to enjoy independence and freedom. It was added that lack of political, economic, social or educational readiness should not be used as a reason to delay independence. Thus, a number of states with low levels of development were born.

Two factors drove Western countries to begin providing aid to these developing countries. First, it was acknowledged that moving from an international order based on colonization and imperialism to one of free trade and fair dealing would require some degree of intervention. In other words, if post-colonial countries were to become trading partners, they needed assistance to reduce poverty and increase productive capacity. Second, Western countries wanted to prevent Third World countries—those neither belonging to the First World (developed, capitalist countries) nor the Second World (socialist countries of the Eastern Bloc)—from drifting towards communism. This fear motivated the development of the Colombo Plan for Co-operative Economic Development in South and Southeast Asia in 1950, which could be considered the world's first development cooperation initiative. The Plan was established to combat poverty in Asia, as it was believed that poverty was responsible for fuelling communist political movements in the region.

Expanding development efforts

The emergence of new international institutions supporting development efforts mirrored the shift in thinking. At the time of its inception, the UN was primarily focused on maintaining peace and security. In fact, the words 'peace' and 'security' appeared in the UN Charter 42 and 148 times respectively, while the notion of 'development' appeared only once. The term 'environment' was altogether absent from the founding Charter (see Box 9).

> **Box 9: Putting the environment on the agenda**
>
> Environmental issues are one example of how the UN has successfully adapted to changing times. Though the environment was absent from the UN Charter and the initial organizational structure, it was effectively integrated into the existing system later on. At the first United Nations Conference on the Human Environment that took place in Stockholm in 1972, the United Nations Environment Program (UNEP) was created as the voice for the environment in the UN system. With UNEP reporting to the GA and ECOSOC, ECOSOC saw environmental issues added to its original mandate of economic and social.
>
> Some argue that the environmental realm needs to be given greater prominence and that ECOSOC ought to more formally recognize it, by, for example, rebranding itself as the Economic, Social and Environmental Council (ESEC) as part of a larger set of reforms. It seems unlikely that ECOSOC will get a new name any time soon, but a 2013 reform of the outdated institution mandated it to convene an integration summit to monitor and promote the balanced integration of the three dimensions of sustainable development (economic, social and environmental). Thus, progress is being made.

In 1945, the UN had just a handful of development-related agencies. The Economic and Social Council (ECOSOC) was created to coordinate social and economic activities within the UN system, while the International Labour Organization (ILO), Food and Agriculture Organization (FAO) and United Nations Educational, Scientific and Cultural Organization (UNESCO) were specialized agencies that fell under ECOSOC's mandate. The following year saw the establishment of the United Nations Children's Fund (UNICEF). However, as preoccupations expanded beyond security issues to areas of development, human rights, humanitarian assistance and the environment, the UN system quickly expanded. During the 1960s and 1970s there was a proliferation of new UN funds, programmes and specialized agencies dealing with poverty and hunger, social development, health, women, environment and housing (see Figure 3). Rather than adding to the mandates of existing agencies, new ones were created.

Figure 3: United Nations Development Group members (excluding regional commissions and Secretariat bodies) by year established

Programme/Fund/Specialized Agency	Year
International Telecommunications Organization (ITU)	1865
International Labour Organization (ILO)	1919
Food and Agriculture Organization (FAO)	1945
United Nations Educational, Scientific and Cultural Organization (UNESCO)	1945
United Nations Children's Fund (UNICEF)	1946
World Health Organization (WHO)	1948
World Meteorological Organization (WMO)	1950
United Nations High Commissioner for Refugees (UNHCR)	1951
United Nations World Tourism Organization (UNWTO)	1957
World Food Programme (WFP)	**1963**
United Nations Conference on Trade and Development (UNCTAD)	**1964**
United Nations Development Programme (UNDP)	**1965**
United Nations Population Fund (UNFPA)	**1969**
United Nations Environment Programme (UNEP)	**1972**
United Nations Office for Project Services (UNOPS)	**1973**
United Nations Development Fund for Women (UNIFEM) (merged into a new organization, UN Women, in 2010)	**1976**
International Fund for Agricultural Development (IFAD)	**1977**
United Nations Human Settlements Programme (UN-HABITAT)	**1978**
United Nations Industrial Development Organization (UNIDO)	1985
Joint United Nations Programme on HIV/AIDS (UNAIDS)	1994
United Nations Office on Drugs and Crime (UNODC)	1997

UN entities established during the 1960s and 1970s to address social, economic and environmental issues

Meanwhile, economic issues such as trade, development lending and monetary policy had been delegated to the Bretton Woods institutions: the World Bank, and the International Monetary Fund (IMF) along with the General Agreement on Tariffs and Trade (GATT). The World Bank and the IMF were established as specialized agencies of the UN, while recognizing that they were independent international organizations. As such, the institutions hold observer status at the UN and are able to participate—though not vote—in the General

Assembly, the Security Council and ECOSOC. The World Trade Organization (which replaced GATT in 1995), on the other hand, is considered a 'related organization' in the UN system, falling under the General Assembly but with no obligation to report to it, and contributing on an ad-hoc basis to the GA and ECOSOC. The relationship between the UN and the Bretton Woods institutions has historically been thorny. Many have argued for the UN to have more authority over economic issues, pointing to the so-called democratic deficit of the World Bank, IMF and WTO, while others support the status quo, maintaining that these institutions are more effective than the UN in achieving their stated objectives.

The North-South divide

Cold War politics saw a political divide between the "East" (the Soviet Union and its allies) and the "West" (North America, Western Europe, Japan, Australia, and New Zealand). With decolonization, developing countries came to outnumber developed countries and the power dynamics shifted within the United Nations as postcolonial countries pushed to have their voices heard. As we saw in the description of the General Assembly, a group of newly independent countries joined forces in the 1950s to push back against the two superpowers—the United States and the Soviet Union. These countries formed the Non-Aligned Movement (NAM) in 1961, what is now often referred to as the "Global South", and many of the same countries also organized themselves into the "Group of 77", to have their economic and social issues heard on the world stage. Despite the breakdown of the East-West divide following the end of the Cold War—to say nothing of the blurring North-South distinction resulting from globalization—both the NAM and the G77 continue to live on.

As Thomas Weiss has pointed out (2011), the "various constructed roles on the international stage in the global theater are played by actors from the two major troupes, North and South". This theater, Weiss argues, is counterproductive to generating universal norms and ensuring human security. Though there are some exceptions, countries have generally adhered to artificial roles based on which side they are on, rather than where they may fall on specific issues. Instead, policy debates should reflect issues-based and interest-based alliances and coalitions.

Millennium Development Goals

The year 2000 was a milestone for development cooperation. For the first time in history, states came together behind a clearly defined set of goals related to social and economic development. The Millennium Development Goals, also referred to as the MDGs, were eight easy-to-remember, time bound, focused and measurable goals that people worldwide could rally behind (see Figure 4). They were drafted in the late 1990s and came into force through the Millennium Declaration, adopted by the UN General Assembly on September 8, 2000. They were intentionally ambitious, with goals such as "halving extreme poverty" and "providing universal primary education" by 2015.

Figure 4: Millennium Development Goals

Source: United Nations

The MDGs were praised for their simplicity. Schoolchildren in Nigeria, Laos and Germany alike could memorize and recite them. They also brought attention to previously under-the-radar issues, like Goal 5 on improving maternal health. Maternal health advocates had long fought for greater attention to the issue, and being given equal presence with priorities such as poverty and hunger, environmental sustainability, and primary education was an important step in mainstreaming it. However, the MDGs were also criticized for being developed without sufficient consultation with key actors, such as UN member states, civil society organizations, NGOs, think tanks and academia. Instead, they were drawn up by a group of experts in a 'basement of UN headquarters'. It is likely that this lack of consultation in the design of the goals meant that developing countries had a weakened sense of ownership of them.

Tallying up the results

> *"The 13 years since the millennium have seen the fastest reduction in poverty in human history"* 2013 UN Report, A New Global Partnership: Eradicate Poverty and Transform Economies Through Sustainable Development

As 2015 approached, the question on everyone's mind was: how successful were countries in meeting these goals? The most impressive achievements were made on fighting extreme poverty. The target to halve the proportion of people living on less than $1.25 a day by 2015 (with a 1990 baseline) was achieved in 2010, five years early. However, this was not the case in all countries, regions, or population groups, but rather on the aggregate or global level. In South Asia the proportion of people experiencing extreme poverty dropped by 41 per cent, while in Sub-Saharan Africa it fell by a mere 14 per cent. Meanwhile huge gains were made in China where the proportion fell from 60 per cent in 1990 to 12 per cent in 2010. Critics noted that China's rapid economic development, which coincided with the timeline to achieve the MDGs but was due to entirely exogenous factors, skewed the overall picture and drew attention away from countries that fared less well.

Significant achievements were made on numerous other goals as well—such as boosting primary school enrolment and improved access to clean water—even if ambitious targets were not always met. The final assessment of the MDGs highlighted that, despite groundbreaking success, millions of people are being left behind, especially the poorest and most vulnerable populations. It pointed to climate change and environmental degradation as factors undermining progress achieved, and stated that conflict remains the biggest threat to human development.

Sustainable Development Goals

A changed world

Long before 2015 approached, the international community was looking ahead to the post-2015 development agenda. The idea for a new set of goals that would replace the MDGs was formally tabled by Columbia and Guatemala at the Rio+20 Summit in 2012, which was the largest summit in UN history. A three-year process engaging millions of people through dialogues, thematic consultations and national surveys culminated in the 17 Sustainable Development Goals (SDGs), also known as the Global Goals, being adopted unanimously by states at the UN Sustainable Development Summit in September 2015 (see Figure 5).

The post-2015 consultation process that led to the development of the SDGs sought to address many of the shortfalls of the MDGs, while also adapting to a new era. When consultations were launched in 2013, the world had become more complex and the discourse around development had changed drastically. The MDGs felt outdated.

Figure 5: Sustainable Development Goals

Source: United Nations

For one thing, the MDGs were meant for developing countries, and funding was to come from developed countries through their official aid contributions, known as Official Development Assistance (ODA). Yet by the time stakeholders were discussing the SDGs, it had become apparent that the traditional North-South lines were blurring. South-South cooperation was becoming a new norm and the economic and political power was beginning to shift from developed countries toward emerging economies, in particular the BRICS (Brazil, Russia, India, China and South Africa). It was also recognized that every country, not just those belonging to the Global South, had room for improvement.

Meanwhile, development finance was becoming increasingly complex and ODA was no longer viewed as the only source of funding to achieve the goals. A number of other sources of finances such as domestic resources (taxation), investment and remittances were gaining relevance and in some cases outpacing traditional aid. For example, as migrant workers went abroad in search of economic opportunities, remittances—money that foreign workers transfer to an individual, usually a family member, in their home country—came to compete with international aid as one of the largest financial inflows to developing countries. In 2000, remittances to developing countries totalled $120 billion (OECD 2006), while by 2015 they had grown to $441 billion (World Bank 2015). Meanwhile, official development aid, or ODA, grew at a much slower pace during the same period, from $80 billion to $147 billion (Compare Your Country).

The world had become less state-centric too. Non-state actors such as the private sector and civil society were playing a more central role in promoting global cooperation and development. Sub-national governments (e.g., provincial, municipal) were also much more involved.

Finally, the global distribution of poverty shifted during the past couple of decades. In 2000, poverty was mainly regarded as an issue for low income countries, with the greatest portion of world's poor in these countries. In 1990, there were 1.6 billion poor people in low income countries, representing 95 per cent of the world's poor. Yet by 2012 when the SDGs were being developed, many of these low income countries had graduated to middle-income status and the number of poor people in low income countries had dropped to 0.3 billion (FUNDS 2016). It was thus argued that inequality and redistribution in all countries needed to be given greater weight. The SDGs reflected this by having a goal devoted to reducing inequalities.

Several other issues addressed by the SDGs but not the MDGs include good governance, respecting human rights, climate change, and peace and security as fundamental to development. These additions are mostly a reflection of emerging challenges and an evolution in thinking about development issues. For instance, climate change is a global threat that became widely recognized only after the MDGs. The same can be said about the linkages between development outcomes and peaceful and just societies. The other reason for certain additions was pressure from stakeholders to include key issues that the MDGs neglected (e.g., secondary/post-secondary education, governance, and energy).

More voices at the table

Quite unlike the process to establish the MDGs, the post-2015 development planning favoured a participatory, consensus-based approach that included years of consultations with tens of millions of people. Consultations consisted of three separate streams. First, UN country teams in coordination with other key stakeholders facilitated 88 national consultations in countries where the UN provides assistance. Second, UN agencies worked with national governments and other stakeholders to conduct 11 thematic consultations. Both of these channels used numerous methods of outreach, including face-to-face meetings, online mechanisms and door-to-door surveys. Lastly, views from the public were sought online through the MYWorld survey. The survey asks individuals to choose six issues that matter most to them and their families from a list of 16 (e.g., affordable and nutritious food, better transport and roads, political freedoms). This survey continues to collect votes and in March 2017 had over 9.7 million votes.

According to Amina Mohammed, special adviser to the UN Secretary General on post-2015 development planning, about 70 per cent of those consulted were under 30 years of age and at least 8 million were contacted through social media.

With regards to the process, Ms. Mohammad states: "[Developing the MDGs] was just a bunch of technocrats sitting round a table to produce a set of goals based on what UN agencies had been doing over the years. There was no attempt to be transformative. For me, the SDG process has been one of the most intellectually and politically and technically challenging endeavours I have ever engaged in."

A summary of how the SDGs differed from the MDGs is provided in Figure 6.

Figure 6: Key differences between the MDGs and the SDGs

	MDGs	SDGs
Timeframe	2000-2015	2015-2030
Scope	8 goals 18 targets 61 indicators	17 goals 169 targets 230 indicators
Target	Developing countries only	Universal
Process	UN-led with little input from external stakeholders or the public	Consultative, participatory, concrete role for civil society organizations

Despite the inclusive and consultative approach taken to their development, the SDGs have not been without criticism. Following the announcement of the new goals, many voiced discontent with their broad scope, calling the 17 goals and 169 targets "dizzying" and "worse than useless". Economist William Easterly suggested SDG stood for "senseless, dreamy, garbled". Many argued they are aspirational and unrealistic, while lacking the precision and clarity needed to be measurable. That these two realities go hand in hand should not be a surprise—the trade-off between the number of parties involved in negotiations and the usefulness of the outcome is an oft-cited challenge in international relations. The process vs. product trade-off is seen across the UN system. It is most pronounced in comparing the Security Council and the General Assembly: the former is known for being an exclusive club of member states but more effective decision making and less watered-down products, while the latter for greater participation but an inability to produce meaningful outcomes.

Financing the goals

A legitimate concern is the high cost of achieving the lofty goals coupled with a lack of adequate financing. It is estimated that meeting the goals would cost $2-3 trillion a year over 15 years, which is roughly 4 per cent of world GDP. Research by Development Finance International suggests that low- and middle-income countries could fund the SDGs if three key sources of public finance were raised: doubling developing country tax revenues; doubling aid flows from developed countries; and raising $500 billion a year from innovative financing (e.g., through introducing taxes or levies on carbon emissions and/or financial transactions and allocating these new monies to achieving the SDGs) (UNRISD 2015).

Currently, none of these financing sources seem likely. Doubling developing country tax revenue would require an increase equivalent to 10 per cent of GDP (ibid). Meanwhile, doubling aid flows would require OECD Development Assistance Committee (DAC) members—the world's major donor countries—to meet their pledge to spend 0.7 per cent of their national income on aid, despite never having met this target since it was agreed upon in 1970. In 2014, the average across DAC members was 0.03 per cent, with only 5 of 29 countries meeting or exceeding the target (Denmark, Luxembourg, Norway, Sweden and United Kingdom) (OECD). Ideas for innovative financing approaches, such as a global financial transaction tax from which revenues would go to achieving development goals, have been proposed for years but have yet to be implemented. The UNDP has also launched an SDG Fund, which, similar to the MDG Fund, is an official funding mechanism in support of the post-2015 agenda. Currently, the Fund's total budget is approximately $60 million (SDG Fund website).

In reality, public funding alone cannot be relied on to meet the financing needs of the SDGs. Blended finance, a concept that seeks to blend public and private capital to finance development goals, has become a new norm. Mobilizing private capital for development-related purposes such as education, health, green technology or microfinance in developing or emerging markets is a promising though still nascent approach to supplementing traditional funding sources. Often referred to as impact investing or social impact investment, capital is typically supplied by financial institutions, investment firms, foundations' endowments, high net worth individuals, pension funds and individual or retail investors. Financial return on investment ranges from below market ("impact first") to market rate ("finance first").

Looking ahead

The new development agenda has been set and implementation is already underway. Attention has shifted to how national governments and other stakeholders will measure progress on the goals and how they will report on that progress. The review process is multi-level and complex. The High-Level Political Forum on Sustainable Development, which convenes annually under the auspices of ECOSOC, is the central platform for follow-up and review of the SDGs. States report to each other at the regional level and regions report to the global level. Each year, the High-Level Forum focuses on a different overall theme and zeros in on a few of the 17 goals. Member states are encouraged to prepare Voluntary National Reviews on successes and challenges related to implementing the agenda. Every four years, the UN Secretariat will prepare a *Global Sustainable Development Report* covering overall trends, and heads of state will meet to review progress.

National governments are thus busy incorporating the SDGs into their national development plans, strategies and budgets, and considering how they will raise awareness and mobilize action among diverse actors. They are not the only ones getting to work. Consultations on the SDGs revealed a strong desire from other actors to be involved not only in the design of the goals, but also in future implementation. What role will the UN play in this next phase and what role will be played by civil society, businesses, and other key stakeholders? Is the UN development system fit to tackle current global challenges in partnership with other sectors? How can it be improved?

Partnering in a new era of development cooperation

The traditional understanding of 'development', a simple characterization of developed-developing, donor-recipient relationships that emerged in the 1960s, is giving way to a new era of universality and global partnerships. The universal nature of the SDGs makes clear that the greatest challenges of our time are not problems of the global South, but global problems. One example is the inclusion of climate change action in the goals. Evidence has emerged that Western, industrialized countries are most responsible for climate change, while its harmful effects have disproportionately affected developing countries that have done little to contribute to it. The goals also recognize that developed countries have a particular duty to ensure sustainable consumption and production, given their sizeable consumption levels relative to poorer states. Reducing income inequality within countries is another example. The level of inequality in the United States—an exemplary country according to indicators related to maternal health, education, preventing and combating disease, extreme poverty and hunger, etc.—exceeds that of many developing countries. Similarly, despite having a much higher Gross National Income (GNI) than most African countries, South Africa is one of the most unequal countries in Africa, and indeed in the world.

Alongside an understanding that current challenges extend beyond developing countries, there is a general acceptance that these broader, more complex problems require new, innovative approaches as well as enhanced collaboration between sectors. Old ways of thinking coupled with a reliance on development aid will not suffice. "Lasting solutions to global problems no longer lie in the hands of governments alone. The United Nations of the 21st century must think in terms of networks and coalitions." (UNSG 2013).

The role of multi-sector partnerships in UN Secretary-General Ban Ki-Moon's special initiatives launched over the past years is telling of the UN's commitment to collaboration:

- **Climate Resilience Initiative,** launched in 2015, seeks to strengthen climate resilience of world's most vulnerable countries and people by "bringing together private sector organizations, governments, UN agencies, research institutions and other stakeholders to scale up transformative solutions." (UN 2015).
- **Global Education First Initiative,** launched in 2012: "a partnership comprised of a range of actors and institutions including governments, UN agencies and multilateral organizations, civil society organisations, and the private sector." (UNESCO GEFI).
- **Every Woman Every Child,** launched in 2010: "an unprecedented global movement that mobilizes and intensifies international and national action by governments, multilaterals, the private sector and civil society to address the major health challenges facing women, children and adolescents around the world." (Every Woman Every Child website).
- **Global Pulse,** launched in 2009: "Global Pulse partners with experts from UN agencies, governments, academia, and the private sector to research, develop, and mainstream approaches for applying real-time digital data to 21st century development challenges." (Global Pulse website).

Analysis of two related UN documents, *The Future We Want* (the outcome document of the 2012 Rio+20 Conference at which the idea for SDGs was officially tabled) and *We the Peoples* (the report proposing the MDGs, released ahead of the 2000 Millennium Summit), demonstrates that the emphasis on partnerships is relatively new. The report published in 2012 cited the concept of partnerships three times more often than the 2000 report did. The term stakeholder(s) was used 26 times in the 2012 report, and only once in the slightly longer report from 2000. Another key document, the UN Secretary-General's 2014 synthesis report *The Road to Dignity by 2030* includes partnerships as one of six "essential elements for delivering on the SDGs". This report mentions partnerships twice as many times as the *The Future We Want* published just two years earlier (Volt 2015).

ECOSOC has placed greater emphasis on leveraging partnerships in support of the international development agenda since 2008 when it began convening an annual Partnership Forum, bringing together governments and stakeholders, particularly from business and foundations, to discuss ways to engage and collaborate to achieve the development goals. At the 2016 Forum, ECOSOC President Oh Joon stressed that governments, the UN system, civil society, the private sector, the philanthropic community and academia must break down traditional silos for more and better cross-sectoral decision-making and solutions (ECOSOC 2016).

Role for private sector

> *"Putting social and environmental purposes in the driving seat of business is the only way to ensure an equitable and sustainable economy for the 21st century."*
> Professor Muhammad Yunus (British Council and SEUK 2015)

The private sector is a critical element in the 21st century notion of partnerships for development. Beyond being a potential source of capital to finance the international development agenda, in itself quite significant, the business world brings expertise, innovation, rigour and efficiency. Businesses and corporations focused on providing technology, products and services to the poor can have huge impacts on poverty alleviation. Think about a company that produces low-cost medical supplies or affordable home water-filters to those at the bottom of the pyramid. Or microfinance institutions, like Grameen Bank or BRAC, that offer micro-loans to the poor who lack access to traditional financial services and would not qualify for a bank loan due to a lack of collateral. Even growing ventures like Lucky Iron Fish, a social enterprise working to reduce iron deficiency in Cambodia and worldwide through a reusable iron fish that can be added to any pot while cooking. The ingenuity and drive of a new class of social entrepreneurs that seek to solve complex social challenges through business is changing the way we think about addressing social issues.

In fact, there is a spectrum of private sector actors that can support the UN's goals. These range from for-profit social enterprises to socially responsible businesses, to corporations looking to engage in corporate social responsibility (CSR) work and purely profit-oriented companies. When incentives align, there is enormous potential for corporations to contribute to meeting the UN's needs while achieving their own social responsibility goals. The UN Global Compact, a voluntary initiative based on business leaders' commitments to adopt sustainable and socially responsible policies, seeks to tap into the booming CSR trend. Self-described as the world's largest voluntary corporate sustainability initiative, it had the participation of over 8,400 companies from 162 countries as of April 2016. This reflects an acknowledgement that global trade, investment and business activity can be powerful drivers of economic transformation and social change. One just needs to compare the $134.8 billion in ODA in 2013 to worldwide trade in goods and services, worth $23 trillion in 2014, to see the potential of a more social impact-oriented private sector (British Council and SEUK 2015). If economic globalization were harnessed for international development, the result would be transformational.

Even corporations not driven by the desire for social change have a place at the table. Public-private partnerships have traditionally been essential to development projects, particularly those related to public infrastructure, transportation, and information technology (e.g., internet access). Recently, interest has broadened to other areas such as affordable or social housing, water and education.

The new attention paid to the opportunities associated with private sector involvement in development outcomes has led to concerns around the risks posed. Many have pointed to the need to ensure transparency and accountability, which is now acknowledged in nearly every UN speech that stresses the potential of private sector partnerships. Accountability is an issue as corporations often have an incentive to keep information confidential in order to protect any competitive advantages. As well, corporations are accountable to their shareholders, not stakeholders, and have a fiduciary responsibility to maximize profits. Inclusion of all relevant stakeholders is not a given. In fact, despite the UN framing public-private partnerships as a way to enhance inclusion of diverse actors, evidence suggests that work in this area remains to be done. Several studies have shown that such partnerships have failed to achieve inclusive participation, particularly of certain groups such as farmers, workers and trade union, indigenous peoples, women, youth or children. If business interests are put ahead of the UN's interest to advance the internationally agreed development agenda, the UN will risk losing its legitimacy and credibility in the eyes of the people.

Ultimately, what is required for these partnerships to be successful is for there to be proper due diligence screening, clear partnership principles and guidelines, and monitoring and evaluation mechanisms to ensure that expected results are achieved.

Role for civil society

Amidst all the promise of leveraging the private sector as a force for good, civil society has been sidelined and its contribution undervalued. That corporations are relatively new actors in this space is partially responsible for the hype. As well, the financial resources they offer are welcome at a time when developed countries are facing recession and cutting their ODA budgets accordingly. Yet civil society, made up primarily of NGOs but also social movements and networks, has been pivotal to advancing the UN development agenda over the past decades.

At the founding conference of the United Nations in San Francisco in 1945, around 1,500 participants from NGOs joined the 5,000 government delegates, members of the media and other officials and staff in attendance. NGO participation at UN world conferences and summits has risen dramatically since. Over 17,000 NGO participants took part in the 1992 Earth Summit in Rio, and in 2012 at Rio+20 the number reached more than 40,000. At the same time, the number of NGOs that enjoy consultative status with ECOSOC has risen from 41 in 1946 to 4,189 today, reflecting both the expanding number of NGOs globally and the greater influence they hold in the UN development arena.

NGOs and civil society organizations are uniquely placed to support governments and the UN in achieving social and economic development, gender equality, environmental sustainability and human rights, as they typically share the same vision and ideals. They achieve impact through knowledge, expertise, lobbying, advocacy, research, priority setting, media outreach and monitoring. They have succeeded in raising public awareness of issues, shaping public opinion, norm setting, influencing international deliberations and negotiations, and pressuring states and the corporate world to be more responsible and accountable. During the climate negotiations in Paris in 2015, civil society movements and self-organizing networks were crucial in getting states to take action against climate change. Their immense contribution to the creation of the SDGs helped ensure an inclusive decision-making process and goals that ultimately reflected the world's most pressing needs.

Through campaigning and political pressure, NGO coalitions played a central role in the adoption of international bans on landmines, ending apartheid, and establishing the International Criminal Court, among many other achievements. With the internet's ability to rapidly mobilize global supporters around an issue or concern, NGOs that make effective use of new technologies have been able to reach the public like never before. Avaaz, the world's largest online activist network, has over 44 million members worldwide. Launched in 2007, its model of internet organizing engages citizens around the world to take action on pressing global, regional and national issues through signing petitions, funding media campaigns and direct lobbying, and organizing "offline" protests and events.

Though technology is enabling civil society organizations to achieve unprecedented scale, NGOs have also increased their impact through partnering or forming coalitions with other NGOs. In global decision-making processes such coalitions are favoured as they are seen to represent agreement and consensus around specific issues. Yet this pressure for a single voice poses a challenge for NGOs, which are as diverse as the problems they were created to solve and the constituents' views they give voice to. This is especially true for NGOs from the South, which tend to be less established and powerful than their Northern peers. Reaching consensus and getting others on board has historically been easier for Northern NGOs than Southern ones, which can mean that voices from the North may be more likely to be heard (Browne and Weiss 2014: 200). This is problematic as NGOs in the South have distinct priorities and interests.

UN leaders have for decades proclaimed that NGOs and civil society are vital to human progress. Former Secretary General Boutros Boutros-Ghali called NGOs "an indispensable part of the legitimacy" of the United Nations. Similarly, Kofi Annan referred to NGOs as "the conscience of humanity" and Ban Ki-Moon said that "civil society has never been more important or needed" (UNSG 2013). Yet despite these declarations, civil society participation in global governance at the UN is not as strong as it could be and NGOs are too often perceived as a nuisance. The following chapter on human rights explores this challenge in greater depth, as NGOs have less influence in the current Human Rights Council than in its predecessor, the Commission on Human Rights. The hostility towards NGOs within the walls of the UN mirrors the fraught relationship between civil society and national governments. In many countries—from those in the global South to the North, from authoritarian regimes to developed democracies—NGOs are increasingly being targeted by governments. Turkey is just one example; its government shut down hundreds of NGOs following the failed coup attempt in July 2016, and international aid organizations helping Syrian refugees in Turkey are experiencing hostility and expulsion (Sanchez 2017).

A number of reforms have been proposed to strengthen civil society's involvement and influence in UN processes. Key recommendations include: establishing permanent, more inclusive structures and mechanisms for civil society participation in institutional decision-making; allocating more funds for relations with civil society organizations; cultivating positive attitudes towards civil society; and increasing the UN's capacity to engage with civil society through staffing decisions, training and guidance. As well, the UN should actively encourage the participation of underrepresented NGOs, with a particular focus on empowering NGOs from the global South that may struggle to attract levels of international attention similar to their Northern peers.

Going forward, civil society and NGOs will be essential to effective global partnerships for development. States recognize that their success will remain limited without the support of civil society, while the business community struggles with accountability. Civil society cannot be marginalized by global actors looking to new solutions to solve the world's most pressing challenges. Their place at the table can contribute to more effective global governance by ensuring a diversity of views and interests.

Innovation and technology

The digital revolution and the spread of mobile technology have transformed international development efforts. The internet and social media have fostered the swift mobilization of people and resources in an unprecedented way. New technology and new applications of existing technology have made possible significant improvements in the developing world across diverse sectors such as banking, education, health and agriculture. Access to technology is not yet universal, but uptake is rising exponentially.

Innovation for development is the latest trend. While the focus here is on the potential of tools such as social media, mobile technology, crowdsourcing, big data and open data, the concept is much broader. It refers to doing things differently, with an emphasis on achieving better outcomes through evidence-based decision making, experimentation to determine what works, scaling successful models and adopting a human-centered design approach.

Mobilizing civil society

One outcome of the internet's penetration in developed and developing countries alike has been a new form of civic engagement. Self-organizing networks and online social movements have succeeded in mobilizing previously unfathomable numbers of people to support causes, pressure governments and corporations, contribute resources, and coordinate action. Social media has been instrumental in enabling the shift from state-based institutions and forums directing change towards a model based on leadership from civil society and other non-state actors. Leading up to the 2015 UN Climate Change Conference in Paris (COP21), individuals and civil society groups expressed their discontent with the inability of states to take action on climate change. Six months before the Conference, over 20 million people had joined the Climate Reality Project and other self-organizing networks pushing for action against climate change (Tapscott 2014). Ultimately, states agreed on a far more ambitious deal than ever before, restoring some degree of faith in the ability to states to act, though the considerable pressure from civil society was undoubtedly a crucial factor contributing to COP21 success.

Fundraising

Social and environmental causes have embraced the internet for its fundraising potential. A particularly striking example was the ALS Association's Ice Bucket Challenge, which dared people to post videos of having ice water dumped on themselves, and challenging others to do the same. It exploded in July and August 2014 and in less than three weeks the ALS Association—a non-profit health organization that few had heard of before the challenge—had raised $15.6 million. The crowdfunding industry, of which social impact initiatives make up a rising proportion, grew from $16 billion in 2014 to an estimated $34 billion in 2015, surpassing the venture capital industry which invests an average of $30 billion each year (Barnett 2015). Online platforms for microfinance lending have also gained momentum in recent years. Kiva, the most prominent platform, has nearly 2.5 million users and has lent over $846 billion to individuals in 84 countries through its field partners.

Sectors: banking, commerce, disaster response, education

Technology has had a tremendous effect on the banking and commerce world, reducing transaction costs and facilitating participation of marginalized populations in global trade. Kenya's mobile money-transfer scheme, M-Pesa, allows people to make microfinance loan repayments, pay bills and send remittances to family members back home using their mobile phones, saving time and money. The cashless nature of electronic transfers also helps reduce theft. In April 2016, M-Pesa had about 19 million active users in Kenya, more than two thirds of its adult population, and over 6 million subscribers outside of the country in Africa, Asia and Europe (Ochieng 2016). East Africa is now regarded as a global leader in mobile banking. Meanwhile, the growth of e-commerce has removed barriers for entrepreneurs to participate in global markets and sell their goods or services to businesses and consumers around the world.

In the field of disaster response, crowdsourced data and geographic information system mapping have drastically improved abilities to respond to natural disasters and other crises in a timely and effective manner. Following the devastating 2015 earthquake in Nepal, Kathmandu Living Labs developed crisis map QuakeMap to better match relief efforts with the needs of affected people and communities. Similarly, HaitiData makes public geospacial maps of Haiti, containing a wealth of information and data to support policy makers in post-earthquake reconstruction. These technologies have applications in other areas as well, such as climate change adaptation and mitigation.

Online learning and massive open online courses, referred to as MOOCs, are innovations disrupting and creating opportunities in higher education. MOOCs first entered the scene in 2008, but gained worldwide attention and praise (along with some criticism) in 2012. Several top US universities, including Stanford University, Princeton, MIT, and University of Berkeley, introduced MOOCs at that time, and hopeful observers envisaged vast numbers of students in developing countries benefitting from the highest quality of education. The hype was not entirely overblown; enrolment began to spread from the West to the rest, emerging countries such as India and Brazil saw homegrown MOOCs take off, and higher education has indeed become more accessible and affordable for everyone. The spread of MOOCs in the developing world is not without challenges, namely that many lack the basic level of education and literacy required to benefit and advantages of face-to-face interaction with professors are lost, but potential is great.

There are numerous other sectors, such as health and agriculture, where information and communications technology (ICT) has been altering the status quo. In terms of making progress on the SDGs, effectively utilizing new technology will be key. As this chapter has explored, social media outreach was instrumental in ensuring that the SDGs reflected the diverse voices from around the globe. Moving forward, data collection through mobile devices and crowdsourcing will be essential to monitoring achievements and progress on the goals.

A main caveat to the great promise that technological advancements hold for accelerating global change is that information and communication technology infrastructure is still lacking in many parts of the world, particularly in rural communities. While access to modern technology varies greatly within countries and according to certain demographics, the digital divide is particularly stark between developed and developing countries. Another risk may be referred to as the "dark side of ICT", when new technology and social media platforms are harnessed to advance global threats, such as terrorism, human trafficking and cybercrime. In recent years we have sadly witnessed that ICT can just as easily be used to reverse social and economic progress as it can be to accelerate it.

What role for the UN?

The changed development landscape has already begun to put pressure on the UN development system. With a multitude of new actors involved, a shift in the nature of poverty, and a reduced portion of ODA being channelled through the UN (a mere 16 per cent of ODA to least developed countries came from the UN in 2012, down from 25 per cent in 1990), the UN needs to consider what its role in development will be moving forward. Overall, its development function appears to be losing relative importance when compared to other UN functions such as peace and security, human rights, and humanitarian aid. With numerous previously low-income countries having graduated to middle-income status, countries have greater capacity to solve their own challenges, and technical assistance is less needed outside least developed countries and fragile states. Yet a different type of support will be sought.

The UN's greatest strength lies in its ability to convene diverse stakeholders and set global standards and norms. It succeeded in consulting a broad range of actors to establish a post-2015 development agenda by and for 'the people'. The challenge ahead will be implementation. Given the centrality of multi-stakeholder partnerships to the UN's plan for implementing the SDGs, the UN will need to ensure that efforts of diverse development actors are aligned with the objectives of the international development agenda. As the primary body for coordinating sustainable development, ECOSOC should play a leadership role in setting global norms. It could start by establishing the principles and guidelines that govern the partnerships. To ensure a convergence between UN and business interests, it could also ask companies engaged in partnerships with the UN to commit to the UN Global Compact Principles.

Actions need to be based on the right intentions, but they also need to be coordinated. To enhance coordination, UN agencies and programmes could be assigned as Task Managers for each SDG. A meta-partnership could then be created for each target which would oversee the contributions of various parties towards the targets and report back to the appropriate Task Managers (Dodds 2015: 13). The UN will also be looked upon for leadership in overseeing SDG monitoring and review, which will take place at the national, regional, and global levels.

Is the UN prepared?

There is little question that the task at hand is a mighty one. In a post-2015 era, the UN is expected to lead in implementing the sweeping and ambitious new development agenda, manage multi-stakeholder partnerships, adapt to a rapidly evolving development landscape, embrace technology and innovation, and measure and evaluate progress.

Yet the UN development system (which refers to the 30+ organizations in the UN system mandated to work in areas related to social-economic development) struggles to remain relevant. The system is fragmented and exists in silos, there is significant overlap in the work of organizations with similar mandates, software and business practices used are as numerous as organizations, and competition for limited resources is rife. Moreover, ECOSOC, the coordinating body, is known for being ineffective and cumbersome.

Meanwhile, the World Bank, which is a specialized agency of the UN, and regional development banks (e.g., the African Development Bank, the Asian Development Bank), which are not part of the UN system but coordinate closely with it, are seen by many experts as the true leaders in development, producing superior research and policy, and operating more efficiently. The UN development system risks being marginalized by other actors if it continues to put off much-needed reform.

Ban Ki-Moon made reference to the shortcomings of the UN development system on multiple occasions, and called for swift action. He reinforced that sentiment in a 2015 statement to the Security Council, stating that “the 2030 Agenda calls on us to move from silos to synergy, to move from fragmentation to partnership.” This recognition that the UN development system requires reform to operate more efficiently and effectively is not new. Numerous attempts at reform have been made, including efforts to streamline the entire system, coordinate the work of multiple UN programs in a given country, and improve how ECOSOC operates. The three key reform initiatives have been the 1969 capacity study which sought to address fragmentation of the development system, Kofi Annan's resident coordinator initiative in 1997, and the 2006 High-Level Panel on UN System-wide Coherence. Yet results have been limited and observers continue to stress the urgent need for more ambitious reforms such as the creation of UN Women (see Box 10).

Streamlining the UN development system and 'Delivering as One'

In the UN's early days, its development work was carried out by a few specialized agencies. During the 1960s and 1970s there was a proliferation of organizations in the UN development system, which today boasts 30 organizations plus research and training institutions. These organizations are headquartered in 16 countries, with over 1000 field offices dotted around the globe. The system has become extremely complex and inefficiencies abound. Some of the challenges associated with having so many players in the system include duplication in policy advice and on-the-ground service delivery, lack of coherence and consistency across the UN system, and competition for funds among UN agencies. For instance, the Future UN Development System, or 'FUNDS' Project, an NGO devoted to accelerating change in the UN development system, points out that there are 16 UN organizations carrying out water and environmental projects.

Box 10: UN Women

In July 2010, the General Assembly decided to establish UN Women, a UN entity for gender equality and the empowerment of women by merging four existing entities dedicated to women: the Office of the Special Adviser on Gender issues and Advancement of Women, the Division for the Advancement of Women of the Secretariat, the UN Development Fund for Women (UNIFEM) and the International Research and Training Institute for the Advancement of Women.

In this rare move of merging entities with overlapping mandates, the UN demonstrated that solutions to an increasingly fragmented and uncoordinated system are possible.

The need for a more robust overall approach has been understood for years. In 2006, Secretary-General Kofi Annan launched the ambitious Delivering as One initiative, following recommendations by the UN Secretary-General's High-Level Panel on UN System-wide Coherence, a group that had been exploring options for strengthening and modernizing the UN system. The objective was for the UN system to "deliver as one" at the country level. Most developing countries have numerous UN development organizations present (e.g., UNDP, UNICEF, FAO, WFP), each with their own office, budget, programme and so on. Through the "Delivering as One" approach, each country sought to improve service delivery and collaborate as one UN team based on One Programme, One Leader, One Budget and One Office (the four overarching principles set out by the High-Level Panel). It was believed that such a unified approach to delivery would reduce duplication, fragmentation and competition for funds, while enhancing capacity for strategic approaches (United Nations 2012: 8).

When it was launched, the governments of eight countries jumped on board, volunteering to become pilots: Albania, Cape Verde, Mozambique, Pakistan, Rwanda, Tanzania, Uruguay, and Vietnam. These pilot countries were encouraged to innovate and experiment with new approaches to collaboration based on the four 'Ones'. During implementation two additional concepts—One Voice and One Fund—were added. The pilot phase concluded with an independent evaluation conducted in 2012 of achievements across the six Ones. Conclusions were mixed. The most positive finding was a strong increase in national ownership and leadership, whereby UN programming in pilot countries was being driven by their own needs and priorities. The greatest challenge proved to be achieving efficiency gains and reduced transaction costs, mainly due to the persistence of overlapping or incompatible reporting requirements and regulations of organizations. This failure revealed the barriers to experimentation that pilot countries face, pointing to the need for more systemic changes at headquarters level.

As of 2016, 52 countries have formally adopted the Delivering as One approach. Most are low and middle income countries, with a handful of upper middle and high income countries as well. To date, progress has remained slow and the UN has not demonstrated leadership in accelerating the process of achieving a unified approach at the country level. This view was reflected in the results of a 2014 survey conducted by FUNDS that asked over 3,200 people from across sectors who interact regularly with the UN which changes in the UN Development System should be implemented by 2025. Many respondents wanted to see changes that are consistent with the Delivering as One" agenda, with the top suggestions including fewer organizations, a single country programme, a single head of the UN Development System and single country representatives for the system.

Improving business practices

The UN system is large and unwieldy, not to mention notoriously inefficient. The top ideas for reform identified by experts in the above-mentioned 2014 FUNDS survey were in fact related to technology, administration and information management. Over 90 per cent of respondents agreed or strongly agreed with suggestions to cut costs and improve efficiency through greater use of technology; develop a single UN gateway to all UN research and publications; and use a common, system-wide technology platform for administration.

Currently, virtually every UN organization and agency uses its own enterprise resource planning software to manage its business activities, service delivery, technology and human resources. Harmonizing business practices across the system and adopting a single platform for all administration would significantly reduce costs and increase the likelihood of delivering through a single office at the country level (which continues to be improbable with the multitude of platforms).

Focusing on strengths and priorities

There is little doubt that some organizations and agencies within the UN development system are far more successful at achieving their stated objective than others. Thus any claims about the effectiveness of the UN development system as a whole fail to account for variation by organization and by sector. For example, the fields where the UN development system is seen to excel are health, education and gender. Similarly, the organizations that are viewed as most effective are WHO, UNICEF, UNAIDS, WFP and UNDP. It is worth noting though that while the UN is generally seen to be a leader in health, its reputation is stronger for achieving long-term impacts than for dealing with pandemics (see Box 11). The areas in which the UN is perceived to be least relevant are crime prevention, drug control, and financial stability (FUNDS 2014). In assessing where to allocate energy and resources, the UN should focus on areas where it has a comparative advantage.

In addition to assigning resources based on relative strengths, the UN should also critically assess how its current programmes and funds fit with the 2030 Agenda for Sustainable Development, and make adjustments as necessary. There are a number of priorities on the agenda where the UN currently lacks expertise and has not allocated sufficient resources, such as urban design and sustainable cities, ocean health, and clean energy. New UN programs may need to be established, while others should be combined or done away with altogether.

Box 11: Global health crises—Ebola response

The Ebola outbreak in West Africa in 2014 and 2015 was among the largest health emergencies the world has faced in recent years. During the two years, the uncontrollable spread of the deadly virus caused more than 11,300 deaths, most of which were in Liberia, Sierra Leone and Guinea. The World Health Organization was widely criticized for its delayed and inadequate response. An independent panel selected to assess the WHO response to the epidemic charged the agency's culture and politics with its poor response, calling for a transformation of WHO's organizational culture and delivery approach, as well as changes on the part of member states.

A key finding of the Panel report was that WHO has a "technical, normative culture, not one that is accustomed to dealing with such large-scale, long-term and multi-country emergency responses occurring at the same time". Lacking a culture of rapid decision-making, WHO "tends to adopt a reactive, rather than proactive approach to emergencies". This contributed to WHO's unnecessary deferral in declaring a public health emergency. Another factor behind the delay was that it did not wish to challenge national governments of affected countries who initially denied the extent of the outbreak due to fears of economic and trade implications. Even when it did recognize the extent of the crisis, a lack of funding for emergency response posed real challenges. At present, assessed contributions account for less than 25 per cent of WHO's biennial program budget; the remainder comes from voluntary funds from donors. While donors do provide a considerable amount of money for emergencies, WHO has no core funds for emergency response (the outbreak and crisis response budget line).

If WHO is to increase its effectiveness in dealing with future pandemics and improve its governance of the entire global health system, it needs to learn from past mistakes and make the reforms necessary for it to be a true leader.

Source: World Health Organization 2015

ECOSOC reform

As we saw in the first chapter, ECOSOC is the principal body for coordination, policy review, dialogue and recommendations on economic, social and environmental issues. Established by the UN Charter in 1946, ECOSOC coordinates the work of many UN agencies and bodies, and acts as a forum to discuss the issues falling within its broad mandate. The Council's membership has expanded over the years, from 18 in 1946 to the current 54 states, elected by the General Assembly for overlapping three-year terms.

ECOSOC has received more than its fair share of criticism. Prominent diplomats, politicians, policymakers and researchers alike have called it a weak and irrelevant institution. Various reasons for this have been put forth, including: an overly expansive agenda that overlaps with that of the General Assembly; a lack of authority or "teeth"; a disregard for results and outcomes; and an unrealistic workload with too many bodies reporting to it. Critics point to a need for ECOSOC to be less bureaucratic, more action oriented and policy relevant.

While many complain about its ineffectiveness and limited ability to exercise authority, there is little consensus around what to do about it. Indeed, some experts have argued that membership is too large and should be reduced, while others have called for a slightly expanded membership. Some feel that certain minor tweaks would do the trick, yet others make a compelling case for a complete overhaul of the institution. Ambitious proposals envision ECOSOC as a more powerful body, capable of making binding decisions rather than merely recommendations. Many observers support the idea of elevating ECOSOC's status to that of the Security Council, which, despite its challenges with representation and fairness, is highlighted as a model in terms of its decision-making authority. Global economic policy coordination features in many reform proposals as well. In the socio-economic development space, the "institutional division of labour" is such that the UN leads on peace and social concerns; the IMF on finance and macroeconomic management; the World Bank on development lending; and the WTO on trade. Certain proponents of a strengthened ECOSOC have argued that the Bretton Woods institutions and the WTO be made more democratic, reintegrated into the United Nations system and subjected to ECOSOC's overall policy coordination.

Under pressure, ECOSOC has attempted to revive itself through several reforms over the years. The early 1990s saw several tweaks, including replacing biannual sessions with one more substantive annual session that had three segments: a high-level segment, a coordination segment, and an operational segment. Member states began sending higher level officials to attend, reflecting renewed interest in ECOSOC's work. In 2006, the General Assembly adopted another resolution (61/16) on strengthening ECOSOC. It mandated ECOSOC to review progress made in implementing the outcomes of UN conferences and summits, including the MDGs. It also gave the Council a greater role in monitoring trends and progress in international development cooperation and offering policy guidance and options to improve effectiveness.

In 2013, ECOSOC again underwent reforms, this time with the aim of making it a more issues-oriented body capable of overseeing implementation of the 2030 development agenda. Among other changes, the Council was mandated to provide greater leadership and guidance on substantive priorities by convening a separate segment on integrating the economic, social and environmental dimensions of sustainable development. In the same vein, ECOSOC began hosting an annual partnership forum in 2008 to explore how multi-sector partnerships can advance global development, as well as an annual youth forum in 2012 to promote youth engagement and the inclusion of key priorities for youth in drafting and implementing the development agenda.

Relative to most reform proposals put forth by experts, these adjustments are fairly minor, and will lead to incremental rather than transformative change. Still, efforts to reform show a willingness on the part of the UN to respond to criticism. However, the absence of a broad consensus around fundamental change demonstrates how complex the issues are.

Is reform possible?

There is a general sense of optimism around the UN's standing, with 86 per cent of programme country governments considering it to be a more relevant partner than two years ago (United Nations Secretariat 2015). And no matter how difficult reform may be, many also believe that it is possible. In the 2014 FUNDS survey of individuals from private sector, UN organizations or agencies, national governments/public sector, academia or NGOs who are familiar with the UN's work, over three quarters said they felt that the UN development system was capable or strongly capable of significant reform. This is encouraging, given the pressure on the UN to deliver on the ambitious 2030 development agenda. ECOSOC and all UN entities active in the development space still have much work to do to prove they are up for the task.

Chapter 4 – Promoting and Protecting Human Rights

Human rights: one of the UN's great ideas that too many countries fail to respect

The fundamental paradox

The protection and promotion of human rights is among the most controversial issues at the United Nations. In a world where states (as opposed to other levels of government or non-state actors) are the central unit, it is they that must protect the rights of their citizens. Yet it is states that are the primary violators. Attempts by the international community to intervene in a given country in order to protect the rights of individuals or groups are often met with accusations of interference with the principle of sovereignty and nonintervention. Indeed, the prevalence of state sovereignty as the guiding norm in international relations remains the greatest obstacle to realizing universal human rights.

Human rights are intended to be universal legal guarantees protecting individuals and groups against actions which interfere with fundamental freedoms and human dignity. They are considered to be inherent to all human beings, whatever our nationality, place of residence, sex, national or ethnic origin, colour, religion, language, or any other status. The defining characteristics of human rights are that they are: universal, internationally recognized, legally protected, equal and non-discriminatory, inalienable, interdependent and indivisible (see Box 12).

Human rights featured prominently in the UN Charter. The Charter begins with a series of pledges: to save succeeding generations from the scourge of war, to maintain compliance with international law, to promote social progress and to "reaffirm faith in fundamental human rights, in the dignity and worth of the human person, in equal rights of men and women and of nations large and small". This strong commitment to human rights and the dignity of each individual came after the devastating loss of tens of millions of lives and human abuses during the Second World War.

But the notion that individuals have basic rights precedes the UN Charter, and even early international cooperation efforts. The UK Bill of Rights was adopted in 1689, the US Bill of Rights which came into effect in 1791, and France's Declaration of the Rights of Man and of Citizen, adopted just after the revolution and establishment of the first French Republic in 1789, are early examples of human rights protection. Historians will trace the origins of human rights ever further back, beginning with the Cyrus Cylinder, an ancient record dating back to 539 B.C. The rights set out in national bills and declarations pertained to civil and political rights and freedoms, and not to what we refer to today as economic, social and cultural rights.

Box 12: Key characteristics of human rights

Universal – The principle of universality has become the cornerstone of international human rights law. It has been emphasized in numerous human rights conventions, declarations, and resolutions, beginning with the Universal Declaration of Human Rights in 1948. All states have ratified at least one of the core human rights treaties and 80 per cent of states have ratified four or more.

Interdependent and indivisible – Human rights can be grouped into civil and political rights, economic social and cultural rights, and collective rights. Certain rights cannot be sacrificed in favour of other rights as all of these rights are interdependent, indivisible and interrelated.

Inalienable – Rights should not be taken away, except in specific situations determined by law and solely for the purpose of securing recognition and respect for the rights of others and of meeting the just requirements of the general welfare, morality and public order in a democratic society.

Equal and non-discriminatory – Present in all the major human rights treaties, this principle prohibits discrimination on the basis of sex, race, nationality, place of residence, national or ethnic origin, colour, religion, language or any other status.

International human rights law

A series of human rights treaties, conventions and declarations adopted since 1945 have given legal form to inherent human rights. Together, these contribute to a strong body of international human rights law. The most significant thus far has been the Universal Declaration of Human Rights, adopted by the General Assembly on December 10th 1948 (which has since been designated Human Rights Day). It was the first international attempt to explicitly spell out basic human rights for all individuals, as the UN Charter did not in fact define human rights. The rights covered can be categorized into various categories: civil, political, economic, social and cultural rights (see Box 13). The Declaration is regarded today as having established the fundamental norms of human rights that we, individually and collectively, should respect and protect.

In 1966, the International Covenant on Civil and Political Rights (along with its two Optional Protocols) and the International Covenant on Economic, Social and Cultural Rights were adopted by the General Assembly, though they only came into force ten years later, in 1976. The two Covenants were in fact completed in 1956 but due to disagreements over definitions, extent and meaning as well as concerns over potential limitations on state sovereignty, it took ten years before they were formally adopted. Even today, not all states have ratified these treaties, including great powers—China is not party to the former, while the US still refuses to become party to the latter. The two Covenants along with the Universal Declaration of Human Rights together form the International Bill of Human Rights. By becoming parties to these and other international treaties, states are, in principle, legally obligated to respect, protect and promote human rights. This means that states cannot interfere with the enjoyment of human rights, they must protect individuals and groups against abuses, and they must take positive action to facilitate the enjoyment of basic rights.

Box 13: Categories of human rights

Civil rights – Both civil and political rights protect individuals' freedom from infringement by governments, social organizations, and private individuals. Civil rights include life, liberty and security; privacy; protection from discrimination; and freedoms of thought, speech, religion, press, assembly and movement.

Political rights – Rights of individuals to participate in politics and civil society such as freedom of association, the right to assemble and the right to vote. Political rights also include procedural fairness in law, including right to a fair trial, due process and legal remedy.

Social, economic and cultural rights – Rights to adequate food, adequate housing, education, health, social security, water and sanitation, work, enjoy one's culture, practice of religion and use of one's language.

There are a total of nine core international human rights instruments. These include the two Covenants discussed above, and an additional seven conventions regarding racial discrimination, discrimination against women, the rights of the child, the rights of persons with disabilities, the rights of migrant workers, enforced disappearance and torture. Beyond the International Bill of Rights and the core human rights treaties, the General Assembly has adopted over 100 other international treaties and declarations addressing a host of issues such as indigenous peoples, marriage, slavery and war crimes. A number of other human rights instruments exist at the regional and national level, which serve to compliment international norms. At the regional level, treaties and other instruments are adopted to reflect human rights concerns specific to a particular region and provide special protection. For instance, the African Charter on Human and Peoples' Rights was strongly inspired by the Universal

Declaration of Human Rights and international treaties, but also demonstrates the African conception of "rights" and the emphasis on individuals' responsibilities. At the national level, when a government ratifies international human rights treaties, it commits to develop national legislation compatible with its treaty obligations and duties. Typically states will do so through adopting constitutions and other laws that formally protect human rights.

Contradictory interpretations

Despite universal human rights norms elaborated in key treaties as well as in the Universal Declaration of Human Rights, a single and consistent interpretation of these rights remains a distant aspiration.

There has traditionally been a North-South divide over the prominence given to various groups of human rights. Western, democratic countries have long stressed the importance of civil and political rights, which deal with liberty and participation in civil and political life. These are sometimes referred to as "negative" rights as the state must refrain from any action that would interfere with individuals' rights and freedoms. Conversely, many countries in the global South have pushed more for social, economic and cultural rights, which are considered "positive" rights as they require the state or other public authority to take positive steps to ensure access to basics such as food, shelter and education. Since negative rights came first, they are called "first-generation", while positive rights which followed afterward are called "second-generation". A third generation later emerged, which focuses on collective or group rights rather than individual ones. The right to self-determination and the protection of groups of persons, such as indigenous peoples, are examples of these "solidarity" rights. In many countries, particularly in Africa and Asia, the emphasis of collective rights over individual rights is reflective of ideologies and values that historically do not regard the individual as the central unit.

States often perceive a trade-off between these different human rights, arguing that certain rights need to be pursued immediately while others can remain on the back burner until the timing is right. Developing countries have argued that the right to development should take priority over other human rights, and that they should be able to neglect certain human rights, namely political rights, as they catch up to the West. Yet this, of course, runs counter to the core human rights principle of interdependence. Stressing the indivisibility of all human rights, the UN High Commissioner on Human Rights recently stated "If States pick and choose which rights they will uphold, the entire structure is undermined." (UN OHCHR 2016).

Cultural relativists have long challenged the notion of universality, asserting that it is a means for the West to impose its values and norms on other countries. While there is a strong case for cultural relativism and the usefulness of considering contextual factors, relativists have seen their cause seized upon by those seeking to justify violations. The latest variant of this has been the emphasis by many countries on the importance of "traditional values". In 2012, the UN Human Rights Council adopted a resolution on "promoting human rights and fundamental freedoms through a better understanding of traditional values of humankind". While it sounds benign, or perhaps even productive, customs and traditions are often cited as justifications by human rights abusers. Consider the practices of child and forced marriages, female genital mutilation, so-called "honour killings", and marital rape that persist in many countries today. Or the countless lesbian, gay, bisexual and transgender (LGBT) people globally who are denied the same rights that others in society enjoy. Traditions have not always been kind to everyone, and in many cases they have indeed impeded people's rights.

The 2012 resolution, which was preceded by two others in 2009 and 2011 requesting further study of traditional values, set a dangerous precedent by creating a potential means through which countries can justify discrimination, harmful practices and other rights violations. Spearheaded by Russia, it had the support of a number of known human rights violators, such as China, Libya and Uganda. Meanwhile those that voted against were mostly Western countries with relatively good human rights records. Former Secretary-General Ban Ki-moon expressed disapproval with this trend on several occasions. At the 2013 International Conference on Human Rights, Sexual Orientation and Gender Identity he stated "I respect culture, tradition and religion—but they can never justify the denial of basic rights." (United Nations 2013).

These varying perspectives reveal that despite a supposedly universal understanding of human rights, what we witness in practice is continuous debate and negotiation around how basic rights are defended.

The tremendous cost of violations

Despite a robust legal and normative framework surrounding human rights, there are numerous cases of human rights violations around the world each and every day. Individuals and groups are denied basic rights to which they are entitled, often by states that have signed and/or ratified human rights treaties.

The current situation in Syria is a particularly appalling. The government has carried out indiscriminate airstrikes in which it has bombed markets, schools, hospitals and clinics, killing thousands of civilians (UNHRC 2017). It has detained people arbitrarily, including many activists, human rights defenders, journalists and humanitarian workers. In early 2017, Amnesty International exposed the Syrian government's secret campaign of mass hangings and extermination, in which as many as 13,000 people, most of whom were civilians believed to be opposed to the government, were hanged at Saydnaya

Prison between 2011 and 2015 (Amnesty International 2017). The Syrian government is believed to be responsible for killing scores of civilians in numerous chemical attacks against its own people, including those in August 2013 and April 2017 which attracted international attention and condemnation. Not surprisingly, Syria continues to refuse to grant the UN access.

This case is far from isolated. When the UN tries to investigate alleged abuses, states are often uncooperative and claim interference with sovereignty. In his opening remarks at the Human Rights Council session in September 2016, the UN High Commissioner on Human Rights, Zeid Ra'ah Al Hussein, expressed grave concern over attempts by countries to block human rights scrutiny. He stated that "monitoring activities, and advocacy intended to help better protect the people of your countries, are refuted as somehow violating the principle of state sovereignty—or even the UN Charter", adding that credible statements by the Office of the High Commissioner for Human Rights are often dismissed as 'biased', 'irresponsible', 'misleading' or based on 'false' premises by countries. A number of countries were singled out for preventing the UN from conducting independent and impartial investigations into alleged abuses, including Syria, Venezuela, Turkey, Ethiopia, Mozambique, Gambia, India, China, Nepal, Iran and the United States.

Unfortunately, this lack of willingness by many states to cooperate with UN human rights observers is correlated with a large number of violations globally. Some examples of human rights issues in the world today are outlined in Box 14.

It would be wrong to assume that human rights violations only occur in non-Western countries, particularly undemocratic regimes. The example of the United States' use of torture on prisoners illustrates that abuses can certainly occur in Western, liberal democracies. Following the 9/11 attacks and increased concern with the threat of terrorism, the United States used "stress and duress" interrogation techniques on prisoners in Afghanistan and in Guantánamo Bay, Cuba, and subjected detainees in Iraq to torture and cruel treatment. The United States Senate report on the CIA Detention and Interrogation Program released in 2014 concluded that "the program caused immeasurable damage to the United States' public standing, as well as to the United States' longstanding global leadership on human rights in general and the prevention of torture in particular." (Senate Select Committee on Intelligence, 16). The 2015 Universal Periodic Review of the US' human rights record similarly suggested tremendous room for improvement.

Box 14: Select examples of current human rights issues

Lesbian, Gay, Bisexual and Transgender (LGBT) rights – There are 76 countries around the world (mostly in Africa and Asia) that have anti-gay laws, a clear violation of basic human rights. A number of these are passing or attempting to pass even more draconian bills. In 2013, an Anti-Homosexuality Act was passed in Uganda that broadened the criminalization of same-sex relations including life imprisonment (the original bill proposed the death penalty). Meanwhile Indonesia, where homosexuality is not illegal, made international headlines in early 2016 after a series of attacks against members of the LGBT community, including by prominent public figures.

Freedom of religion – Sadly, religious minorities are often the victims of violent attacks. The Muslim minority in the majority Buddhist Burma and Hindu and Christian minorities in the predominantly Muslim Pakistan are but a couple of examples from a long list of cases where individuals and groups have come under attack based on their religion. In Saudi Arabia, conversion from Islam to another religion is punishable by death and the government provides no legal recognition or protection for freedom of religion.

Freedom of speech and press – Too many countries today are guilty of denying people basic freedoms of expression. Security and intelligence forces in Iran have arrested journalists, bloggers and social media activists, who were given heavy sentences. The Chinese government notoriously censors all forms of media, communication and education, including the internet, television, film, literature and video games. Russia has also suffered a worsened reputation recently for intensifying its harassment and persecution of critics and activists.

Use of torture, ill-treatment of detainees and enforced disappearances – The United States' detention facilities at Guantánamo Bay in Cuba came under intense fire for human rights abuses including the use of torture. In its effort to combat organized crime, Mexican security forces have been involved in countless violations including extrajudicial killings, enforced disappearances and torture. Among numerous other abuses, Egyptian officials have in recent years committed torture and enforced disappearances, and mistreatment of detainees have led to many deaths.

The United Nations' Record in Upholding Human Rights

The organizational structure of UN organs, offices, agencies, treaty bodies and committees charged with ensuring that states apply human rights norms is complex and dizzying. Though not an exhaustive list, some of the main ones are: the Security Council, the General Assembly, the Human Rights Council, the Office of the High Commissioner for Human Rights, the International Court of Justice, the International Criminal Court, International Criminal Tribunals, treaty bodies and various committees on specific areas of concern such as the rights of the child, torture and discrimination against women.

An assessment of the overall impact of the UN's human rights work reveals that it is particularly effective at promoting and developing human rights, but is failing to adequately protect those rights when countries opt not to respect their obligations. This stems from a reliance on political and diplomatic processes as the means to achieving its objectives. Such an approach works for offering resources and technical assistance to countries, which in its very nature is non-confrontational, but has posed significant challenges when intervention is required to protect individuals from abuses (Freedman 2015: 54). Politicization is a defining feature across the human rights machinery; one that has hindered its success for decades. Selectivity and bias are widespread, and national interests consistently triumph over principled action. Diplomacy favours dialogue and cooperation, which rarely produces results where grave violations have occurred. An utter lack of enforcement mechanisms across UN human rights bodies has worsened the problem. Unlike domestic laws, international laws are often not enforceable. The international community can apply pressure to uncooperative states through tools such as sanctions or military invasions, but aside from these extreme measures and simple diplomatic pressure, sovereign states cannot be obliged to do anything.

The following section examines the complex system of human rights bodies at the UN, including their strengths and weaknesses and proposals for reform. It focuses on the bodies exclusively concerned with human rights and humanitarian affairs, though it is worth noting that much of the work of the General Assembly and Security Council centres on human rights issues. Through setting standards and passing resolutions to condemn or draw attention to human rights violations, the General Assembly's role in advancing human rights is mostly an indirect one. The Security Council plays a more central role, holding the authority to reach a binding "decision" that a situation is a threat to or breach of international peace and security. It has occasionally done so during particularly serious human rights abuses. We do not provide a detailed account of how these two UN organs have defended or failed to defend human rights. Suffice it to say, they have been plagued by some of the same challenges as the UN's principal human rights bodies explored below, namely the primacy of power and politics. Meanwhile, innovations in the human rights field such as the Responsibility to Protect norm and the International Criminal Court have emerged largely to provide limits to sovereignty, which continues to dominate both the General Assembly and the Security Council.

From the Commission on Human Rights to the Human Rights Council

When the Human Rights Council replaced the Commission on Human Rights in 2006, observers hoped that it would not suffer from the same defects as did its futile predecessor. Established in 1946 as the UN's principal mechanism and forum for the promotion and protection of human rights, the Commission had a 70-year run marked by a few early successes followed by countless challenges. During its first 20 years it successfully established the international legal framework outlined earlier in this chapter. It was also responsible for the many conventions adopted over the years.

Having succeeded in setting norms and standards for states to follow, it shifted its attention in the late 1960s to monitoring and implementing human rights. This meant going beyond simply elaborating treaties to investigating, reporting on, and condemning violators. This new focus quickly turned political and states viewed it as infringing on the principle of sovereignty. It soon exposed the inherent contradiction between the political nature of the Commission (it was, after all, a body made up of member states that represented their own national interests) and its mandate to act for the principled protection of human rights.

A main criticism of the Commission was that its membership included known human rights abusers. The complete absence of membership criteria beyond geographic composition meant that not only did the body not select members based on an exemplary human rights record, but nor did it exclude states with appalling records. At the time of the Commission's collapse, Sudan enjoyed membership despite the genocide taking place in Darfur, as did Zimbabwe while the Mugabe government pursued forced evictions and demolitions that left 700,000 people homeless and created a "humanitarian crisis of immense proportions" (Hoge 2005). This had been an issue for years but worsened in the early 2000s. The straw that broke the camel's back and ultimately led to the demise of the vexed human rights body was the election of Muammar Gaddafi, the Libyan leader whom many labelled as a dictator and tyrant, as chair of the Commission in 2003. Over time it became clear that human rights abusers were actually seeking membership on the Commission as a means of protecting themselves from closer examination. And since violators were less likely to condemn other violators, their presence further threatened the body's credibility.

The political nature of the Commission led to marked regionalism and group-blocking action. Regional alliances that were particularly visible were the G77, the Non-Aligned Movement, and the Organization of the Islamic Cooperation. Members were frequently encouraged by regional allies to vote against resolutions about grave violations in order to protect group members. In a flagrant show of contempt for the Bush administration, the Muslim-African bloc voted the United States off the Commission in 2001, while countries like Sudan and Pakistan were elected as members (Freedman 2011: 35). In many instances, regional alliances and friendships overrode misconduct because membership is decided by votes from the world's regions.

Country-specific resolutions were the primary mechanism for addressing human rights abuses in countries. They became highly political weapons used by states to shield allies from scrutiny as well as to disproportionately lambast opponents. The United States would frequently focus on human rights violations in Cuba but stay silent on more serious abuses in allied states like Guatemala and El Salvador. During the Cold War, the Soviet Union similarly used human rights as a political tool when it criticized rights violations in Chile under Pinochet (an ally of the US), while ignoring the grave human rights situation in communist states (Weiss et al. 2014: 211). Too often, states' actions revealed political motivations and obvious double standards.

The Commission was ultimately scrapped and replaced with the Human Rights Council following former Secretary General Kofi Annan's recommendation in a 2005 report. It was believed that the challenges with politicization and selectivity were so great that a complete overhaul was the only option for reform. But the ensuing discussions around what a more effective human rights body would look like proved more difficult and divisive than expected. First, there was no consensus on the optimal size of the Council. Annan suggested limiting membership to 15, while others wanted it to be universal. Nor was there agreement over what, if any, membership criteria should be established. Many developing and non-democratic nations already saw human rights as a Western tool being used against them, so the idea of excluding violators and undemocratic states would have only acted to reinforce this belief. And creating an exclusive club of likeminded, Western countries would have likely led to further polarization between the two groups. As well, given the variation in states' understanding of human rights that was explored earlier in this chapter, it would have been near impossible to settle on any common definition of a 'tolerable' human rights record to begin with. As a way to promote the primacy of human rights over politics, the notion of having human rights experts rather than government representatives on the Council was discussed. However, many states were not willing to concede power and see the new body become an expert rather than political one.

In the end, after a great deal of deliberation, the newly established Human Rights Council did not differ greatly in architecture, function or composition from the ineffective Commission: it has 47 rather than 53 members, no membership criteria is used, and representatives are government officials concerned with national interests. It was not identical to the Commission and introduced some new features explored below, but it was unable to tackle the heart of the issue. It is therefore little surprise that the Council has fallen short of expectations.

The Council did not get off to a good start. During its first year in 2006, China, Russia, Egypt, Cuba and others were elected as "champions". The US decided not to even run, but rather to be an observer, as a means of protesting the UN's inability to address the flaws of the Commission, especially the membership of human rights violators. After two years it withdrew altogether (though under Obama the US reversed this decision of the Bush administration, running and getting a seat in 2009). Politics were omnipresent. The first session saw Israel condemned nine times, yet no other country. Over the Council's first four years, six of the 12 special sessions that members held were focused on Israel. During the same period, the human rights situations in Myanmar, Darfur, the Democratic Republic of Congo and Sri Lanka were the subject of a single session each. There is little doubt that the Council has maintained the Commission's strong bias against Israel. And while later sessions centred on Syria and other countries, it is still too early to proclaim a permanent shift.

The 2016 Human Rights Council election saw several countries with less than stellar human rights records elected or re-elected as members, including China, Egypt, Cuba and Saudi Arabia. This points to the continued need for some minimal criteria for membership beyond the current *voluntary* pledge stating that the country will uphold international standards of human rights and listing their actions in advancing and protecting human rights. In the absence of strict guidelines, the international community may in some cases decide itself that a country is not worthy of a seat on the council. We witnessed this in October 2016 when Russia was defeated in its bid for re-election. But this is only possible when a regional group puts forward more candidates than the number of seats available, as was the case in Eastern Europe where Russia, Croatia and Hungary competed for two seats. There was no such competition for Saudi Arabia, a country that had been indiscriminately bombing civilians in Yemen during the 18 months prior to the vote. Given that the Asia group had put forward just four candidates—Saudi Arabia, China, Iraq, and Japan—for four seats, it came as little surprise when they all won. Despite the predetermined results, Abdullah bin Yahya Al-Moallami, the Saudi Ambassador to the UN, still claimed that "the re-election of Saudi Arabia reflects the international community's trust in the pioneering and leading role of the Kingdom in the Human Rights Council." (Saudi Press Agency 2016). This potential to bypass a competitive process needs to be addressed for the Council to maintain its credibility.

The Council has enjoyed some achievements, alongside criticisms. Not unlike the Commission, its greatest strengths lie in setting international standards and norms, raising awareness on human rights issues, and convening actors at global forums. It has fared even better than its predecessor when it comes to considering the human rights situations in specific countries, particularly through the Universal Periodic Review mechanism that emerged from the reform process. Each year the human rights situation in 42 countries is reviewed, meaning every country gets its turn every four and a half years. The process requires countries to submit a 20-page report on their efforts to improve human rights and overcome any challenges to the enjoyment of these rights. To reduce bias, two supplementary reports are submitted alongside the "national report". The first contains the views of Special Procedures (i.e., independent human rights experts), human rights treaty bodies, and other UN entities, while the second includes information provided by NGOs and national human rights institutions. Discussions are held and an outcome document is drafted with recommendations for states. Once adopted, states are expected to confirm which recommendations they accept. It is fairly rare that states reject recommendations, with the acceptance rate at 70-90 per cent (Ramcharan 2011). Whether countries implement the recommendations remains to be seen, but it is encouraging that the Universal Periodic Review has been fairly well received by states. Its universal nature has meant that all countries are treated equally, while the emphasis on dialogue over the naming and shaming has reduced impressions of being targeted or singled out.

Diagnosing a problem can be infinitely easier than developing a good solution. Despite this, there is no shortage of proposals for improving the flawed human rights body. A number of workable ideas are outlined in the final chapter. But reforming the Human Rights Council will certainly not be straightforward, especially if the reform process of the Human Rights Commission is any indication.

The Secretary-General and the High Commissioner for Human Rights

Not all parts of the UN human rights apparatus are as political as the Security Council, General Assembly and Human Rights Council. At the opposite extreme are the UN treaty-based bodies, which are the least politicized, biased and selective. These bodies are comprised of experts rather than government officials and do not have jurisdiction over states that are not party to the relevant treaties. They serve to monitor the implementation of key conventions and protocols. There are 10 such bodies, including the Human Rights Committee (monitoring civil and political rights), Committee on Economic, Social and Cultural Rights, Committee on the Elimination of Discrimination against Women and the Committee against Torture. Somewhere in the middle are the secretary-general and the High Commissioner for Human Rights. Both roles require a careful balance of impartial human rights advocacy and political sensitivity. Failure to advocate for principled human rights protection would result in criticism from human rights NGOs and commentators, while neglecting politics would lead to a loss of support of member states.

There has been tremendous variation in the degree of outspokenness of past secretaries-general. Typically the world's top diplomats have prioritized progress on peace and security over human rights, presumably to reduce the risk of offending states by singling them out as violators. Kofi Annan, a vocal human rights defender, was a notable exception. He used his position as a means to push states to behave better, albeit he did so cautiously. His successor Ban Ki-moon spoke out about some grave violations, but was fairly non-confrontational and would usually defer public statements until major powers had taken stances (Weiss et al. 2014: 204).

The job of the High Commissioner for Human Rights is particularly demanding. The General Assembly created the post in 1993 following a successful lobbying campaign by several actors including many NGOs, the Carter Presidential Centre and the US government (ibid: 207). Earlier that year, the UN Vienna conference on human rights had also recommended it be created. Unlike with the secretary general who juggles multiple priorities and can choose not to make human rights a prime concern, the high commissioner enjoys no such luxury. Ruffling some feathers is effectively in the job description for this key human rights post. This sheds light on why so many who have assumed the position have been harshly criticized, even to the point of having to step down. This was the fate of the former president of Ireland Mary Robinson who was nominated as high commissioner for human rights by Secretary-General Annan. After Robinson drew much public attention to human rights violations in China and Israel, the US, which had close relations to these states and preferred quiet diplomacy to public condemnation, grew disillusioned with her and pressured her to resign in 2002. Louise Arbour, who assumed the post in 2004, also became disliked by Washington over time, while her successor Navanethem (Navi) Pillay upset many governments by highlighting violations against LGBT people and by focusing on specific abuses in Rwanda, Sri Lanka and Syria (ibid: 208-9). Since accepting the role in 2014, Prince Zeid Ra'ad Al Hussein of Jordan denounced violations in many states. Prior to Donald Trump's election in the US, Zeid called him "dangerous"—a rare move for his office and one that suggests further clashes with Washington are to come (Cumming-Bruce 2016).

Dealing with the worst violations: the International Criminal Court and ad hoc tribunals

Crimes against humanity, war crimes and genocide represent the most heinous human rights abuses. What distinguishes these 'international crimes' from other violations of human rights is that they are widespread or systematic attacks knowingly committed against a civilian population. Crimes against humanity can include murder, extermination, enslavement, deportation, torture, apartheid, imprisonment, enforced disappearances, and other offences if they are committed on a large scale against a population that is predominantly civilian. Unlike war crimes, they can take place either during a time of peace or of war. As their name would suggest, war crimes can only occur during conflict, and are violations of international humanitarian law or the law of armed conflict. Many of the offences are similar to those categorized as crimes against humanity, though it also covers areas like hostages and prisoners of war. Genocide occurs when an intentional attack is carried out to destroy a national, ethnic, racial or religious group (United States Institute of Peace).

International criminal courts and tribunals have been established to prosecute individuals who, in committing these grave crimes, violate international criminal law. The Tokyo and Nuremberg trials were the first tribunals created to prosecute and punish those guilty of international crimes. After the Second World War the world was appalled by the atrocities that had taken place. Military commanders and political leaders in Nazi Germany were guilty of crimes against humanity, war crimes and genocide. Since there was no body of international criminal law at the time, it was effectively 'invented' and 'applied retroactively' to ensure the crimes committed did not go unpunished (Freedman 2015: 29). International criminal law later became codified and incorporated in international, regional and national law. A number of international criminal tribunals and special courts have since been set up after wars and mass killings to bring justice to victims and deter others from committing such crimes. Criminals were prosecuted for genocide and crimes against humanity through tribunals in Rwanda and the former Yugoslavia, while special courts in Sierra Leone, Lebanon, Cambodia and East Timor dealt with serious violations in those countries.

The ad hoc nature of these tribunals and courts was the impetus for the eventual creation of a permanent court, the International Criminal Court (ICC). Based in the Hague, the Netherlands, the ICC is the first-ever permanent, treaty-based court of its kind that hears cases against individuals (the International Court of Justice is also a permanent, treaty-based international court, but only deals with disputes between states). It cooperates with the United Nations while remaining formally independent from it. The ICC was born through the Rome Statute adopted in 1998, but only began work formally after the Statute had entered into force in 2002. It has 18 judges elected by states parties for a term limited to nine years, no two from the same country.

The ICC does not have universal jurisdiction to investigate any situation it pleases; rather, states decide to be bound by the Court's rules by signing and ratifying the Rome Statute. For countries that are party to the Rome Statute, situations may only be brought to its attention when national courts are unwilling or unable to prosecute individuals. As such, the Court was designed to complement existing national judicial systems. Crimes in non-party states that remain outside of the Court's jurisdiction can still be investigated if they are referred to the ICC by the Security Council. Similar to the courts and tribunals that came before it, a main objective of the ICC is deterrence—stopping leaders from believing they can get away with heinous crimes.

Since its inaugural session in 2003, the ICC has opened ten investigations and publicly indicted 39 individuals, including Ugandan rebel leader Joseph Kony, Sudanese president Omar al-Bashir and Libyan leader Muammar Gaddafi. Its first judgement was issued in 2012 when it found Thomas Lubanga, Congolese rebel leader, guilty of war crimes related to child soldiers. Several others have been found guilty since. Aside from the most recently opened investigation in Georgia, every case investigated has been in Africa, and all 39 people indicted have been Africans. This prompted a perception among African countries in particular that the court is biased against them. In October 2016, three African countries—Burundi, Gambia, and South Africa—announced that they would withdraw from the ICC, becoming the first countries to do so. In explaining his country's decision to leave the Court, Gambia's Information Minister Sheriff Bojang described the global judicial body as "an International Caucasian Court for the persecution and humiliation of people of color, especially Africans" (Sieff 2016). Many observers fear the decisions to leave will spark a mass exodus of African countries. Already Kenya and Namibia's parliaments have voted to withdraw, while Uganda's president has harshly criticized the Court, even calling it "useless" (Gaffey 2016).

Whether the ICC is biased against Africa has been the focus of much debate. The challenge with such a claim is that many of the cases that have been investigated were referred by African governments themselves—34 of which are members of the ICC. The situations in Sudan and Libya, countries that are not party to the ICC, were referred by the Security Council. So when the Court is accused of discriminating against Africa for not investigating situations in other countries, it is a criticism that should in fact be directed toward the Security Council. The ICC Prosecutor did cause an upset when on his own authority he decided to investigate post-election violence in Kenya, effectively challenging the Kenyan government which objected to the decision. However, this case was the exception rather than the rule. Electing an African Prosecutor, Fatou Bensouda of Gambia, in 2011 to replace the Luis Moreno Ocampo of Argentina helped combat anti-Africa perceptions to some degree. And looking at the preliminary examinations currently underway (in the pre-investigation phase), many are in countries outside Africa, including in Afghanistan, Colombia, Iraq/UK, Palestine and Ukraine.

Since its inception, the much-needed human rights institution has struggled with the consequences of states being allowed to choose whether to opt into the ICC or not, as many have chosen not to. Before any country had announced it would withdraw, 124 states were parties to the ICC. If a state decides not to be bound by the Court's rules, its citizens can avoid arrest and prosecution simply by remaining in their country or not stepping into a country that is party to it. The US, which has been accused of committing war crimes at an Iraqi prison in 2003, has not sought membership in the Court (and with the US holding veto power, the Security Council will not refer this case to the ICC). Neither has Sudan, where the ICC has issued arrest warrants for those allegedly responsible for the genocide in Darfur, including the Sudanese president Omar al-Bashir. Since the country is not party to the ICC, the individuals can only be arrested if they enter a country that is. Even then, the ICC must rely on that country to make arrests as it cannot arrest individuals itself. However when Bashir flew to South Africa in 2015 for a summit, the South African government declined to arrest him. The dispute escalated politically, ultimately leading to South Africa's decision to leave the ICC, a surprise move given it had been a vocal supporter of the Court in its early days. This series of events served as a reminder that even if states join an international organization and agree to be bound by its rules, they can only be encouraged, not forced, to fulfil their commitments.

In addition to the US, several other influential countries have decided not to join including great powers Russia and China. Russia had signed but not ratified the ICC's statute, but in November 2016, a day after the Court classified the Russian annexation of Crimea as an occupation, it formally withdrew its signature. Though significant, the move was purely symbolic, given Russia was not subject to the Court's jurisdiction to begin with. The combination of powerful countries deciding not to join and perhaps more importantly the series of recent departures from the Court have caused real harm to the institution as a body that derives its legitimacy from members' willingness to be bound by its jurisdiction.

When the ICC was established, there was a strong sense of hope among NGOs and UN officials that it would effectively challenge state sovereignty and international politics and put human rights first. Human Rights Watch exclaimed at the time, "The International Criminal Court is potentially the most important human rights institution created in 50 years. It will be the court where the Saddams, Pol Pots and Pinochets of the future are held to account." (Human Rights Watch 2002). Sadly, what we have witnessed instead is that state power and politics have prevailed over attempts to prosecute the worst human rights violators, even where mechanisms to seek justice exist under international law. Until this is addressed, the ICC will remain a flawed institution.

Responsibility to Protect and human security

The Responsibility to Protect, or R2P, norm was a similarly promising innovation in human rights protection. As with the ICC, it was developed in the early 2000s to overcome the principles of non-intervention and sovereignty in the face of mass atrocities. The idea behind R2P was simple. Sovereignty is not a one-way street that leaders can use with impunity. Alongside a state's right to sovereign independence comes the duty and responsibility to protect its citizens from gross violations. If a state proves unable or unwilling to do so, or if the state itself is the perpetrator, the principle of non-intervention yields to the international responsibility to protect. It came about as an alternative to the hotly-debated "humanitarian intervention". In the 1990s, two devastating events—the genocide in Rwanda and war crimes committed during the Kosovo War—had demonstrated the deadly consequences of the UN Security Council's failure to authorize interventions in order to protect civilians. States recognized that the controversial "right to intervene" centred on coercive military intervention needed to be replaced by a more nuanced "responsibility to protect" that framed military action as a last-resort measure and favoured prevention over intervention.

The R2P norm was first articulated in the 2001 report of the International Commission on Intervention and State Sovereignty (ICISS), *The Responsibility to Protect,* financed by Canada for the UN. The report outlined three specific responsibilities of the international community: to prevent, to react and to rebuild. State sovereignty was framed as contingent on meeting certain obligations rather than an absolute right, and the notion of 'human security' was prioritized over state security. Fortunately the report's fate differed from that of many other international committee reports that largely go unread. Instead, the norm was widely acknowledged and quickly gained traction. It was endorsed by the 2005 UN World Summit and included in Kofi Annan's report *In Larger Freedom.*

The issue of ensuring 'right intention' was recognized from the outset. The ICISS report noted it as a precautionary principle, stating, "The primary purpose of the intervention, whatever other motives intervening states may have, must be to halt or avert human suffering." The report went on to propose specific criteria which must be met to justify intervention but these have never been adopted by the Security Council. Thus R2P critics often note the uneven application of the principle, pointing to cases where great powers have used R2P as an excuse to intervene when it has been in their interest to do so, while ignoring grave situations where they stood to gain little or nothing. Commonly cited examples of abuses of the norm include: the US and UK in Iraq in 2003 where R2P was a post-hoc justification for the war after original claims of Al-Qaeda links and weapons of mass destruction fizzled out; Russia in Georgia in 2008 which was inspired by imperial aims more than protecting human rights;

and France's intervention in Burma in 2008 after a hurricane hit and the local government was slow to react (Weiss et al. 2014: 29).

Recent events in the Middle East have reaffirmed that the decision to protect and assist vulnerable individuals ultimately rests on political will and military capacity. In 2011, the Security Council was swift to authorize military intervention in Libya to protect the population from the ongoing atrocities. Meanwhile it has utterly failed to do the same in Syria, where the moral justification for intervention has been at least as strong as it was in Libya at the time (many would argue it has in fact been stronger). A host of factors explain the paralysis over action in Syria: the military challenge was tougher, potential costs of coercion were believed to exceed the benefits, and the geopolitics differed greatly with both Russia and China exercising veto power to prevent action and express their general opposition to foreign intervention (Weiss 2014b).

The intervention in Libya was initially lauded as a successful instance of R2P application. As explained in Chapter 1, a problem arose when the US, UK and France went beyond the Security Council's agreed-upon mandate of limited civilian protection to helping usher in a regime change. This move upset the BRICS states (Brazil, Russia, India, China and South Africa) in particular and contributed to states' unwillingness to respond to the Syrian crisis soon after. It also prompted Brazil to table the "Responsibility while Protecting" (RwP) proposal, which stresses that military action must be pursued as an absolute last resort, and that implementation should be subject to close monitoring and regular review (Evans 2015).

Edward Luck, the UN's first-ever Special Advisor on the Responsibility to Protect (2008-12), reiterated these concerns while reflecting on R2P's first ten years. Despite the wide acceptance of the prevention and protection principles, he stated that questions remain for states on implementation. He noted unfinished business with regard to operational practice, accepting individual responsibility, and developing a more nuanced understanding of sovereignty. Echoing Brazil's RwP proposal, he stressed the need for exercising greater responsibility before and after protecting. According to Luck, a key challenge stems from the 2005 Summit's failure to specify who is responsible for protecting, as individual responsibility can get lost in collective responsibility. "The challenge now is highly political and highly practical. We need to convince national policymakers: (1) that curbing atrocities serves their broader foreign policy and security objectives; and (2) that we know how to do prevention and protection in a cost-effective and sustainable manner." (2015: 503). He makes a useful distinction between territorial sovereignty and "decision-making sovereignty". Few countries have used territorial sovereignty claims to protest against actions under the R2P principle, yet many insist on retaining the right to decide whether and how to act—something he sees as a real stumbling block for the implementation of R2P.

More than a decade after the 2005 World Summit, R2P undoubtedly remains a crucial norm. Evidence of its growing normative traction lies in the general acceptance and support for R2P in both the General Assembly and the Security Council. Between 2005 and early 2011 the Security Council had only endorsed four resolutions mentioning R2P, but between March 2011 and October 2015 it had adopted 31 resolutions that referenced this principle—figures that may surprise some given the strong disagreements over the Libyan intervention in March 2011 and ensuing claims of R2P's demise (ibid). Still, the pillars related to preventing and rebuilding have proven less controversial than that which calls on states to react, thus going against the core norm of non-intervention. And as we have seen, R2P is by no means a guarantee that those in danger will receive assistance; geopolitics continues to dictate who is helped and who is left behind.

Migration, refugees and the humanitarian response

In 2016, the UN reported that the number of forcibly displaced people worldwide—a staggering 65.3 million—was the highest in human history. The previous record had been set in the aftermath of the Second World War. While displaced people refers to refugees, internally displaced persons (IDPs) and migrants, only those in the first two categories are considered to be 'forcibly displaced' (see Box 15).

The conflict in Syria undoubtedly accounts for a large portion of those displaced. Since the civil war began in March 2011, over 11 million Syrians have fled their homes—more than half the population of Syria. Despite a focus on the refugees pouring into Europe, most of those displaced remain in the region. In early 2017, the UN estimated that over 5 million were refugees in neighbouring countries (Turkey, Lebanon, Jordan, Egypt and Iraq) and 6.3 million were internally displaced within Syria (UNHCR 2017). While the world spotlight has been on Syrian refugees, conflict and unrest in Iraq, Libya, Somalia, Afghanistan, Yemen and elsewhere have equally led to an exodus of people from these countries.

Under international law, refugees have the right to safe asylum. This includes physical safety but also freedom of thought, speech, religion and movement, freedom from discrimination and torture, and economic and social rights such as access to health care, education and work. The key legal document pertaining to refugee protection is the 1951 Refugee Convention, which has been signed by 144 states. It defines 'refugee' and spells out their rights, as well as the legal obligations of states to protect them.

Box 15: Key terms related to the movement of people

Refugees – People fleeing armed conflict or persecution by crossing their national border to seek safety in nearby countries. Refugees are defined and protected in international law and the status guarantees access to assistance from states, UNHCR and other organizations. Governments have specific responsibilities towards anyone seeking asylum on their territories, as defined in national legislation and international law.

Internally Displaced Persons – Those who are forced to flee their homes, often for the very same reasons as refugees—war, civil conflict, political strife, and gross human rights abuse—but who remain within their own country and do not cross an international border.

Migrants – Unlike refugees, migrants do not relocate due to a direct threat of persecution or death but rather to improve their lives. Typically they are searching for better job opportunities, but they may also relocate for education, reuniting with family or other reasons. Countries accept or reject migrants based on their own immigration laws and processes.

Stateless Persons – Those who are not recognized as citizens by any state.

The conflict in Syria undoubtedly accounts for a large portion of those displaced. Since the civil war began in March 2011, over 11 million Syrians have fled their homes—more than half the population of Syria. Despite a focus on the refugees pouring into Europe, most of those displaced remain in the region. In early 2017, the UN estimated that over 5 million were refugees in neighbouring countries (Turkey, Lebanon, Jordan, Egypt and Iraq) and 6.3 million were internally displaced within Syria (UNHCR 2017). While the world spotlight has been on Syrian refugees, conflict and unrest in Iraq, Libya, Somalia, Afghanistan, Yemen and elsewhere have equally led to an exodus of people from these countries.

Under international law, refugees have the right to safe asylum. This includes physical safety but also freedom of thought, speech, religion and movement, freedom from discrimination and torture, and economic and social rights such as access to health care, education and work. The key legal document pertaining to refugee protection is the 1951 Refugee Convention, which has been signed by 144 states. It defines 'refugee' and spells out their rights, as well as the legal obligations of states to protect them.

The United Nations High Commissioner for Refugees (UNHCR) is the UN's refugee agency and the guardian of the Refugee Convention. It was established in 1950 to help the millions of Europeans displaced after the Second World War. UNHCR was only meant to exist for three years, and was to conclude its work once it had successfully dealt with the refugee problem in Europe. No one could have predicted that this would not be the last refugee crisis to face the international community. Not only has it been dealt new challenges every few years, but the number of people that fall under its mandate has risen steadily each decade (see Figure 7). Since 2012, the increase has been drastic. The scenes of mass population movements have shifted over time—from Europe to Asia (and to a lesser extent Africa and Latin America) beginning in the 1960s, and then to the Middle East at the turn of the century.

Figure 7: Populations of concern (refugees, asylum-seekers, IDPs, returnees, stateless persons), 1951-2015

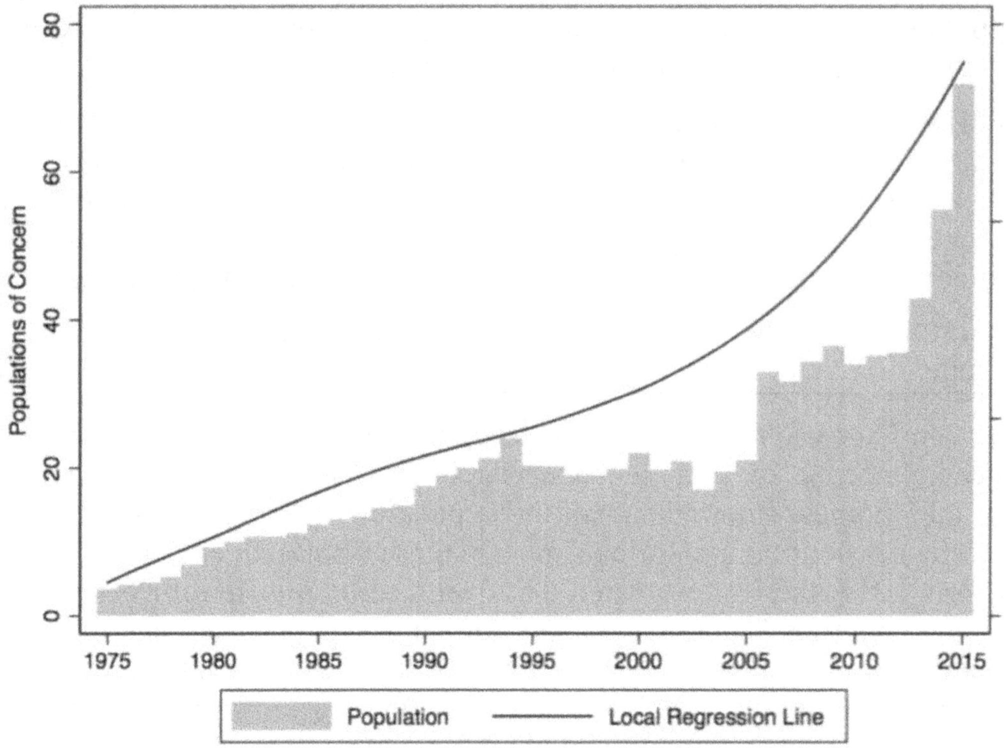

Source: UNHCR data. Available at: http://popstats.unhcr.org/en/overview

The UN is generally well regarded for its humanitarian work and support for refugees. UNHCR has helped more than 50 million refugees since inception and received two Nobel Peace Prizes for its worldwide assistance to refugees. Yet the magnitude of the current emergency has left it overwhelmed and under-resourced. In 2014 the UN's World Food Programme (WFP), which relies entirely on voluntary contributions, ran out of money and food supplies and was forced to suspend food assistance to 1.7 million Syrian refugees. Without a reliable source of funding, it had to resort to online crowdfunding to raise the $64 million needed to reinstate the food vouchers program. The 72-hour social media campaign with the hashtag #AdollarAlifeline was a desperate plea, asking members of the public to donate $1 to the cause (WFP 2014).

It is little surprise that the escalation of the current crisis has led to a renewed discussion around addressing the root causes of refugee movements and mass migration. In his former role as head of UNHCR, UN Secretary General Antonio Guterres was forthright about the need to address this, stating "To those who trigger and prolong conflicts, leaving humanitarians to clean up the mess, it is time to say that this must stop. We as humanitarians can no longer pick up the pieces." (UNHCR 2014). Unfortunately, the UN has had far less success in ending conflict than it has in providing humanitarian assistance and aiding refugees.

The UN has also struggled to get states to do their part in accepting refugees and respecting their obligations outlined in the Refugee Convention. Fears of Islamic radicalization and terrorism have driven nationalism and anti-immigrant public narratives in many Western countries. Some states were reluctant to welcome refugees from Syria and elsewhere in the Middle East, whom they perceived as a greater threat than refugees of past eras.

While the UNHCR has been praised for its work with refugees, the General Assembly has been criticized for failing to get states to make the commitments needed to end the suffering of millions worldwide. The first-ever Summit for Refugees and Migrants was held at the opening of the 71st UN General Assembly in September 2016. Member states adopted an agreement aimed at improving educational opportunities for refugee children and working conditions for displaced adults, while fighting to counter xenophobia and fear. Meanwhile the US convened a Leaders' Summit on Refugees the following day to get individual states to agree to accept more refugees and to encourage states and companies to contribute material support (both funding and in-kind contributions) for refugee assistance programs. NGOs were largely disappointed by the outcome of the summits and human rights critics held that the international community has not done enough. Salil Shetty, the Secretary-General of Amnesty International, stated that, "Faced with the worst refugee crisis in 70 years, world leaders have shown a shocking disregard for the human rights of people who have been forced to leave their homes due to conflict or persecution." (Amnesty International 2016).

In March 2017, Secretary-General António Guterres appointed Louise Arbour of Canada as his Special Representative for International Migration. Having served as UN High Commissioner for Human Rights and Chief Prosecutor of the International Criminal Tribunals for the Former Yugoslavia and Rwanda, Arbour is well placed to lead the follow-up to the migration-related aspects of the 2016 Summit, and to work with member states and other stakeholders to develop a global compact on safe, orderly and regular migration.

What next?

Reforms: big and small

This chapter examined the major failings of the United Nations in protecting human rights globally. Despite having a solid reputation for promoting human rights, specifically in the areas of education, capacity building and technical assistance, the global body has struggled to reconcile its political nature with the principled protection of human rights. A lack of judicial authority and enforcement mechanisms have limited its success. Scholars and experts have put forth many reform proposals—both big and small—to improve the UN's role in advancing human rights worldwide.

A particularly ambitious idea is to establish a World Court of Human Rights that would address the lack of judicial and enforcement mechanisms at the international level to protect individuals from abuses and punish violators.

The scholars behind the proposal, Nowak and Scheinin, argue that there is a gap in the judicial system and many violations of international human rights law raised by individuals (rather than by states) are outside the jurisdiction of existing forums. Indeed, the ICC was created to deal with breaches of international criminal and humanitarian law, but not cases that fall exclusively under human rights law, while the International Court of Justice only hears cases between states. Meanwhile decisions made by UN committees monitoring core international human rights treaties do not carry enough weight to fill the remaining void.

An early vision for a World Court of Human Rights was developed in the 1970s but it took years for the idea to be fully fleshed out. In 2014 a Statute for the World Court of Human Rights (the Treaty of Lucknow) was drafted through an international collaboration of judges, lawyers and scholars. Proponents are currently raising awareness of the project and encouraging states to adopt the Treaty of Lucknow to actualize the Court. They hope to see India and the US agree to champion the new institution (World Court of Human Rights website). Not all human rights commentators are as enthusiastic though. Many express concern that the Statute in its current form does not adequately address the problems that other international legal bodies suffer from, namely whether countries could be convinced to accept the Court's jurisdiction as binding and how it would enforce its judgements.

A range of less radical reform proposals have been put forward over the years. Freedman has suggested that a more practical solution than a World Court would be to strengthen and utilize regional human rights courts. Three of the world's regions have human rights mechanisms: Europe, the Americas and Africa. Each of these mechanisms relies on a regional rather than universal understanding of human rights, which helps explain why compliance has been strong. A similarity in norms, culture, practices and governance has made countries more willing to engage with regional mechanisms than those at the international level. Equally crucial has been the geographic, political and economic linkages that connect countries within a region. These ties often lead to tacit pressure on states to cooperate on human rights, which in turn understand the potential ramifications of noncompliance. To start, Freedman proposes that human rights mechanisms be created in Asia and Eastern Europe, and that pressure be exerted on all countries to join a regional system. Financial aid and technical assistance would then need to be provided to ensure that regional courts could afford acceptable human rights procedures. The pitfall of this approach is that it appears to abandon the aim of truly universal human rights protection.

In an effort not to forgo the notion of universality, observers have offered diverse options for improving the UN human rights machinery. The Human Rights Council, not surprisingly, has been the primary target. The concluding chapter outlines reforms suggested by Bertrand Ramcharan, former acting High Commissioner for Human Rights, which are particularly sensitive to real-world constraints. Schwartzberg (2013) also provides useful ideas for strengthening the essential human rights body. Weiss (2009) blames bureaucracy and lack of leadership for the UN's inaction in situations like the Rwandan genocide, while Hanhimäki (2008) maintains that there are simply too many human rights bodies and that reform efforts should emphasize consolidation. This primer does not intend to explore proposals in detail, but rather to inspire further reading on the topic.

There is clearly no shortage of good ideas, but how likely are we to see reform of the UN human rights machinery in the near future? If the process of replacing the flawed Commission on Human Rights with the Human Rights Council taught us anything, it is that achieving substantial change is no easy task. That colossal effort wrapped up just over a decade ago. Despite underwhelming results, it is doubtful that another ambitious reform will be on the table any time soon. For one thing, doing so would be to admit defeat. As well, overhauling institutions or entire systems is costly in terms of time and resources which could otherwise be allocated elsewhere.

More plausible would be a series of smaller reforms or tweaks that would lead to incremental change in the right direction. Human Rights Up Front, a Secretary-General initiative launched in 2013, is an example of how the UN has sought to improve how it delivers on its human rights mandate through means within its control—in other words, non-Charter, internal reforms. The initiative strives to realize a culture change within the UN system, by increasing awareness among UN staff of human rights and their responsibilities, while encouraging them to take action to prevent violations.

Can change happen?

That the United Nations is merely an organization of sovereign states acting on their own cannot be overstated. As is the case with maintaining peace and security and achieving sustainable development, progress on human rights depends entirely on member states. It would be as unrealistic to expect states to concede power to the UN (or any other global institution) to protect and promote human rights as it would be to hope for a radical shift in attitudes with regards to state sovereignty. Still, states that do not currently prioritize human rights can be swayed over time. A crucial factor in getting states to act is pressure from domestic private groups, foreign NGOs, and international organizations. Whether it is in a liberal democracy or in a repressive government, non-state actors often succeed over time in exerting influence on states to respect human rights.

International human rights NGOs like Amnesty International and Human Rights Watch have been particularly instrumental in supporting the UN over the past decades to protect and promote human rights. Through their work documenting violations, engaging in fact finding and advocating for action, they play a crucial role in exposing abuses and pressuring states to address them. Without their tireless efforts, it is unlikely that the ICC would have been created, or that states would have adopted the International Ban on Landmines when they did. Sadly, many countries—Russia, Turkey and China are particularly prominent examples, but there are countless others—have been increasingly cracking down on NGOs, journalists and the media. When an authoritarian regime suppresses freedom of speech, limits the activity of NGOs and harasses human rights defenders, it makes it more difficult to identify what Freedman refers to as 'hidden abuses'. These unreported or under-reported abuses are taking place around the world, in countries like North Korea, Equatorial Guinea, Gambia, Qatar, Saudi Arabia, and Turkmenistan.

Yet even authoritarian regimes are finding that technology and social media are disrupting their ability to exert absolute control within their borders and dominate the public discourse. In an already complex world of human rights protection, 'citizen journalism' has emerged as a promising mechanism to expose human rights violations, particularly in countries where freedom of press, speech or expression is not guaranteed. During the Arab Spring when foreign reporters were frequently denied access and state-run media served only to spread government propaganda, individual citizens captured abuses with cell phone cameras and shared them on social media websites and blogs such as Facebook, Twitter, YouTube and WordPress.

Some observers believe that human rights protection is shifting outside the realm of the state, as governments find it harder to hold onto their accustomed control. There may be an element of truth to this, but it would be premature to predict the demise of the state.

The subjective nature of human rights complicates matters further. States adopt their own understandings of human rights and choose to prioritize certain rights over others, as this chapter has explored. That they are party to the same treaties and declarations gives a false sense of consensus. Even among otherwise similar states (not to mention within states), disagreements often occur. We have witnessed this in Western states over issues like abortion, banning religious clothing or symbols, and whether health care should be considered a public good. Human rights are matters of moral judgement after all.

Norms do change and adapt in the long run. But until there is actual consensus among states, the UN will find it difficult to provide systematic and authoritative protection. Progress on some fronts suggests there is reason to be hopeful, yet backtracking on others justifiably raises concern. Whereas the overall trend is positive in the areas of peace and security and development, it is difficult to discern with human rights. Although the UN has succeeded in placing the concept of 'universal' human rights on the international agenda, actually protecting human rights still remains as much of a challenge for the UN today as it was in 1945.

Chapter 5 – Workable Global Institutions: How to Get from Here to There?

> *"The Charter of the United Nations frequently maps out a chasm between its aspirations and the means to achieve them. War is to be renounced, human rights are to be advanced, and development to be a priority. Yet peace is beholden to the five permanent members of the Security Council, human rights obligations remain limited to voluntary commitments taken on by states, and development is the paradigm example of an unfunded mandate."* Simon Chesterman (2015: 505)

This book has attempted to show, first, what the United Nations is and does and the astounding contributions it makes to the world. Second, we have tried to explain why the UN is so forcefully criticized for being unable to deal with urgent world problems. Third, we have wanted to indicate the sort of analysis that is required to understand this world institution.

In this concluding chapter we consider possible reforms to the United Nations, building on the analytical foundations that have been laid throughout the book. We begin by looking at what others have been saying about how to approach global reform. Then we list some of the types of reforms that are urgently required. Finally, we analyze how we can bring about global reform. Specifically, how do we get citizens to want to transfer authority to world institutions so that institutional transformation is on the political agenda?

What we have learnt about understanding world institutions

Our goal is to find a possible path toward more workable 21st century global institutions—that is to say, authoritative institutions that the world will obey. What did the history of international organizations and the analysis of their present operations tell us about transforming the UN into an effective global institution? The complex picture is not always clear. Nevertheless, let us draw the best conclusions we can.

If the founding of the League and the UN taught us one thing it is that it took great leadership, diplomacy, and public communication. It took a Woodrow Wilson or a Franklin Roosevelt. They contributed ideas and deep thought, but they were also skilled at selling the concept to the public. Roosevelt dreamt of an organization that could overcome unilateralism, alliances, spheres of influence, and balance of power politics. This did not materialize but the ideals led the way to what was possible. The leaders were backed by solid secretariats, and the impetus and ideas of private individuals and civil society also played a role. So, can we conclude that it takes a great power to lead the way? Perhaps. Certainly, the major powers cannot be opposed. Does it take a specific personality? This is not certain either. Wilson failed to implement the League in the US and Roosevelt passed the baton to his successor Harry Truman, a sound but not a notable leader. There was a definite need for diplomacy and persistence to deal with contradictory goals. Member states wanted both cooperation and independence; internationalism compatible with their national interests; and hierarchy alongside equality and participation. This is exactly the United Nations we got.

Aside from the actors of the moment, the international organizations were also the result of their historical context. The League and the UN would not have come about without the devastation of war. Nor would they have come about without the cumulative historical precedents and models. They were, in part, the result of years of international thinkers, ideas, and conferencing—given birth to by cumulative 'internationalism'. So, we may say that new international organizations resulted from what we have called the 'big bang theory' as well as 'evolutionary historicism'. They were also children of their epoch. They were spawned by the post-war economic, social and technological conditions. Now the question is: are we finding ourselves in a 'global era' corresponding to new 'global' challenges and requiring 'global' institutions?

Our analysis of the United Nations—including its significance, the need for its transformation, proposals for reform, and barriers to achieving them—also provides useful insights when considering a path forward. To begin with, the importance of the UN is enormous. This book has discussed many of its numerous achievements at length. As coordination managers, conveners, and the setter of standards, the UN's contributions to peace are staggering. In 2016 there were 16 ongoing multidimensional UN peace operations with 120,000 military, police and civilian personnel trying to limit conflict in the world. At the same time, the UN is the world's largest coordinator and supplier of humanitarian aid and is responsible for managing the gigantic 2030 Agenda for Sustainable Development (the SDGs). The organization has also been responsible for introducing and mainstreaming new concepts such as human rights, R2P, and gender equality, as explored in *The Power of UN Ideas.* Under Ban Ki-moon's leadership, the UN made great strides in ensuring that climate change would be on the world's agenda, including through convening the successful 2015 Climate Change Conference in Paris.

Just as the need for the UN is evident, so is need for its transformation into an effective global institution. Critics point to the UN's lack of legitimacy as a decision-making body, and the absence of democratic participation and fair representation. The Security Council's two-tier system that accords a veto to the powerful is seen as unequal treatment. Many do not consider its decisions to be moral or justified, not to mention the issue of impasses, when vetoes are used. Meanwhile, the General Assembly that relies on 'one member, one vote' rather than a form of weighted voting is also charged with being unrepresentative. The Human Rights Council struggles to protect human rights globally as it struggles with a fundamental contradiction: it is a political body expected to take principled action. The Economic and Social Council deals with its own challenges, namely being a slow and bureaucratic organization that cannot make binding decisions and whose mandate greatly overlaps with that of the General Assembly. The result has been countless calls for reform of the UN system and the need for a global movement to bring them about.

Beyond simply exposing the weaknesses of our present institutions, our analysis also revealed that there is no shortage of proposed improvements. Many aim to improve representation, fairness and effectiveness of the major organs, particularly the General Assembly, Security Council, ECOSOC and the Human Rights Council. Others focus on issues such as securing adequate financing, autonomous emergency peace services and increased engagement and consultation with stakeholders. Later in this chapter we will go into nine key reform ideas in greater detail.

Despite all the good ideas that have surfaced over the years, we have also seen why the UN's hands are tied and why we are not moving ahead. There is indeed a considerable gap between the ideas for reform and the political will to implement them. Most states do not want a more powerful and effective UN. And although the significant steps taken toward the international responsibility to protect have limited sovereign impunity, we are still living in an era of nation-state predominance. The primacy of national power and politics is hardly disputable. Meanwhile, there has been no sustained campaign to communicate the UN's achievements or to speak of its need for additional authority to deal with global challenges. These are a couple of reasons we have yet to see genuine change.

Reviewing the literature on revamping the UN

> *"To respond to today's and tomorrow's threats to peace and security, the United Nations must become more relevant, more credible, more legitimate and more capable."* Mogens Lykketoft, President of the General Assembly (UN 2016)

Before outlining reform proposals and discussing how to get citizens to want to transfer authority to global institutions, we should take a peek at what various experts have been saying on the topic. In this section we examine three major, recent examples of thinking about revamping the UN.

In *UN 2030: Rebuilding Order in a Fragmenting World,* a 2016 report by Kevin Rudd, former Australian Prime Minister and Chair of the Independent Commission on Multilateralism, 10 principles are put forth for reforming the United Nations in response to the "globalization of everything". To ensure a more relevant and responsive UN, Rudd highlights the need for agenda setting that is future-oriented (dealing with, for example, cybersecurity and lethal autonomous weapons systems) and proposes strengthening policy-planning capability. He argues for breaking institutional silos through a 'Team UN' approach of multi-disciplinary teams dealing with specific challenges on the ground, as well through the structural integration of the UN's peace and security, sustainable development, humanitarian and human rights agendas. To improve member state participation and cooperation, he calls for a formal commitment to multilateralism by member states and for the UN to build bridges between the great powers to reduce tensions. Rudd also suggests a greater focus on prevention, better results management, and enhanced efficiency to deal with the reality of budgetary constraints. Finally, he makes the case that women should be at the centre of the UN agenda and that youth need to have their voices heard in UN councils.

While all this looks like a reasonable agenda for change it should be noted that it is very light on structural modifications. In fact, it looks more like administrative adaptation to the new demands of globalization, most of which is going on to some degree within the UN as it is. Although good principles are announced, there are no institutional changes for bringing them about.

The 2016 report *Reinventing Development: Reforming the UN for People and Planet* by Barbara Adams and Karen Judd specifically warns that institutional transformations that would demand shifts in power structures within the United Nations may take a long, long time. Thus, they claim, efforts aimed at major structural changes may stand in the way of the kind of urgent reforms that can make the UN a more capable force for people and the planet. There are deeply entrenched interests that support the status quo, so it may be more effective to ignore difficult institutional reforms and instead concentrate on the critical issue of development.

According to Adams and Judd, there is already a framework in place for member states to transform the UN. It is composed of the three new global 'agendas' hammered out in 2015 by states and civil society: the 2030 Agenda for Sustainable Development (SDGs); the Addis Ababa Action Agenda on financing for development; and the Paris Agreement on climate change. The agendas reflect a political effort to come to terms with new global realities. They can potentially forge international cooperation under the auspices of the UN. Unlike past development agreements, the 2030 Agenda is universal, thus requiring all countries to measure and report on progress.

The authors point to rising corporate influence and the emerging gap in accountable governance as obstacles to realizing development goals and serving public interests. They explain that universal norms and standards are not applied consistently across the UN nor are they necessarily accepted by other institutions such as the WTO or IMF. Since trade and investment largely bypass the UN, public interest is not always guaranteed. Another challenge they outline is that the UN's assessed contributions have become increasingly inadequate for covering the organization's increased responsibilities.

In order to overcome these obstacles, Adams and Judd list four priorities for member states, which are necessary for achieving the three new development agendas: greater integration of the three pillars of the United Nations (peace and security, human rights and sustainable development); implementing a new funding formula to finance goals and commitments; adopting a values-based framework for intergovernmental processes; and creating a culture of accountability. Taken together, these imperatives constitute an agenda for reform.

All this seems very plausible and reasonable. The question is, of course, will the three agendas be respected without any authority to ensure compliance? Is a bunch of NGOs snapping at the heels of recalcitrant states enough to make them keep their promises? It never has been in the past. Do the three agendas have enough clout to ensure change at the UN? The authors offer good suggestions for achieving these, and the three agendas include timelines and measurable goals. And experts and civil society are working hard to try to ensure states fulfil their obligations. But will 'should' and 'must' become 'shall' and 'will'? Is it just another case of planned reforms without teeth? Will improvements in development spill over into power politics? The fundamental question we have to ask ourselves is whether 'process agendas' can transform international politics without any substantive change to institutional structures and their underlying power imbalance and entrenched interests.

In June 2015, the *Report of the Commission on Global Security, Justice & Governance* was published. It is one of the most significant, recent studies proposing the renaissance of the UN. In presenting their report, Ibrahim Gambari, co-chair of the Commission and former Nigerian Foreign Minister and UN Under-Secretary-General of Political Affairs, noted that "the UN and global governance institutions are ill-suited to address many modern evolving threats and must reform or risk prolonging and deepening global crises." According to the other co-chair, former U.S. Secretary of State Madeleine Albright, the world requires "more capable tools of global governance, with different kinds of public, private, and mixed institutions designed for twenty-first-century challenges."

The report, which is over 100 pages in length, presents a comprehensive agenda for reform. It focuses on the priority objectives of security (specifically state fragility and violent conflict), climate governance, governing the global economy, reforming global institutions, and engaging partners. Some of its key recommendations are summarized below:

- **Security:** The Commission advocates focusing on conflict prevention, strengthening the role of women in peace and security, and building consensus on criteria for determining when to apply R2P. To deal with conflict situations, it calls for enhanced UN capacity in military, police and civilian response, through rapid deployment and military planning, designated military units, state-formed police units, and a standing and reserve capacity of civilian specialists.

- **Climate change:** The creation of a number of new climate change entities is suggested to support the implementation of the COP21 climate commitments. These include: an International Carbon Monitoring branch, a Climate Research Registry, a Climate Action Clearinghouse, and a Climate Engineering Advisory Board. It is also proposes that additional investments be made in climate adaptation and that private enterprise be engaged on market-based incentives to reducing emissions.
- **Governing the global economy:** To foster a renewed framework for global economic cooperation and crisis response, the Commission turns to what it calls the G20+, where the plus signifies enhanced coordination with the UN and Bretton Woods institutions. Interestingly, this proposal comes despite acknowledging a lack of evidence that G20 agreements led countries to reshape national actions in a significant way. Other priorities outlined include: combating illicit financial flows and extremist financing, instituting effective governance of natural resources, and securing the digital economy while promoting internet access in the Global South.
- **Reforming global institutions:** For the General Assembly, its recommendations include streamlining its agenda, leading the post-2015 development agenda and developing a consultative UN Parliamentary Network that would have a formal relationship to the UN as an advisor to the GA. The purpose of the network would be to bring together elected parliamentarians from their national legislatures to discuss and advise on issues of UN governance. It would also function as an additional channel to civil society, and to expand public knowledge and participation in UN work. Regarding the Security Council, the Commission proposes that membership be expanded and immediate re-election of non-permanent members be allowed. It adds that the SC should consult more with civil society and business. On modernizing the Secretariat, it is recommended that the secretary-general selection procedure be improved and that the SG be given more discretion to manage the Secretariat. Other ideas are put forth related to the Peacebuilding Commission, international courts and human rights bodies.
- **Engagement:** The Commission stresses the importance of the UN engaging with critical regional, local, civil society and business actors in global governance.

To realize these changes, the Commission recommends a transitional strategy for reform—a longer-term approach to modernizing global governance structures. Specifically, it calls for the building of 'smart coalitions' to mobilize support to sustain reforms, the convening of a Conference on Global Institutions in 2020, and establishing a mechanism to monitor and coordinate reform.

We can see that there is certainly no lack of proposals for reform in this report. In fact, the Commission's work is an excellent example of combining high-minded analysis of the need for better global governance with its members' judgement of what is actually possible. It is pragmatic, but not at the expense of good ideas and necessary changes. The only caveat is that it could go further in terms of offering ideas for institutional transformation. For instance, it stops short of suggesting an autonomous, emergency peacekeeping force or independent funding sources for the UN. Finally, in devoting the last chapter to "Getting from Here to There", the report goes further than most in setting us on the path to thinking about *how* we can achieve reform.

Nine popular proposals to transform the UN

To conclude this book, we present in greater detail a list of widely-known proposals for strengthening the United Nations before terminating with a set of ideas about how the renaissance of the UN can be brought about. To guide the process of understanding and contextualizing these proposals, we begin by offering some reflections on the various types of change (with their corresponding level of ambition) along with contrasting approaches to achieving change.

It is helpful to think about change in terms of different gradations. It has been said that reform falls into two categories: a more up-to-date alignment of status and authority and better management of the system (Fasulo 2015: 237). But, in fact, it is a little more complicated. First, there are simple adjustments to administrative, financial, personnel and budget considerations—often called 'reform'. These may be purposeful, managed improvements to administration. The UN has been quite effective at this sort of continuing reform. The terms 'reform' and 'change' can cause confusion as they are often used as catchall terms to include the whole spectrum of change at the UN. Second, we have 'adaptation'. This refers to modifications made on an ad hoc basis to deal with short-term problems, without any overall plan or purpose. Third, a more fundamental form of change is what is called 'transformation'. Transformation entails structural modifications to the composition, organization, norms and rules of an institution to allow it to better cope with the effects of socio-economic, technical and political change. It may question the goals, purposes, values and functions of organizations. This is sometimes referred to as changing the 'architecture' of the international system. Far more than a merely academic question of definitions, the terms 'reform', 'adaptation' and 'transformation' are critical to our understanding of what we are trying to achieve (for an elaboration, see Trent 2007: 24-30).

Once the desired change is determined, there are multiple strategies that can then be considered for how to achieve such change. Reformers (and we hope this will include you) struggle over whether to aim for radical and immediate change, or for incremental steps that may amount to a transformation over time. In historical terms the debate has been over revolution or evolution—what is theoretically necessary or what is politically attainable. In the first chapter we introduced this debate, concluding that the founding of the League and the UN were the result of both 'big bangs' (the world wars) and 'historical evolution' (a cumulation of progressive steps).

On the one hand, a gradual approach to change that considers political constraints can be seen as practical and realistic. The hope is that smaller, achievable changes will eventually lead to a larger shift. We recall this recommendation from leading scholars when it comes to improving the Human Rights Council.

The challenge is that these minimalist arguments may focus on what is probable at the expense of what is desirable and what may, at a future time, be possible. Ambitious dreams for an alternative world order are often driven down to the lowest common denominator by those counselling practicality and prudence. Reformers must be inspired by the vision of a cooperative world, as were the founders of the League and the UN. This means being challenged by the end target of workable institutions that can respond to the challenges of tomorrow. It means being animated by the goals at the tip of our grasp while accepting all practical steps to move ahead.

So perhaps the two are not irreconcilable after all. As Ban Ki-moon wisely put it: "Keep your head above the clouds, and your feet firmly on the ground. And move up, step by step. That means: Dream big—but be practical." (UNSG 2016).

Finally, a brief note on how we selected these nine ideas. We must stress that all the following proposals have their critics. They are also not intended as an exclusive plan for revamping the United Nations, but rather examples of reforms that could allow the United Nations to gain legitimacy and develop the institutional capacity to make respected, authoritative decisions. Each of the proposals is what we call "workable", meaning it is practical, necessary and can be implemented. However, unlike the lists prepared by various international commissions and high level panels, our choices are not the proposals that might be considered the most politically acceptable. They are instead based on what is necessary to make the UN a credible global institution that can give leadership to the world. They range from grandiose to minute.

1. A more legitimate Security Council

One fairly radical but 'workable' proposal for restructuring the Security Council is made by Joseph Schwartzberg in his powerful book, *Transforming the United Nations System: Designs for a Workable World.* He recommends a three-pronged approach. First, to surmount national interests and help smaller countries to work through larger groupings, he suggests a system of representation in the Council by 12 world regions rather than individual nation-states.

Each multinational region would nominate slates of candidates from which one would be elected to the Security Council by the General Assembly. Second, he proposes a mathematically determined weighted vote for each region. Third, in exchange for phasing out the veto, the P5 would be rewarded with a larger weighted vote in a more empowered General Assembly.

Additional new proposals for reforming the Security Council have been made in the 2015 *Report of the Commission on Global Security, Justice and Governance.* To achieve the twin goals of effectiveness and acceptability, it is suggested that the Council's membership be expanded to reflect the tremendous increase in UN membership (as was done in 1965) and that immediate re-election of non-permanent members be allowed. The Commission then proposes ideas for resolving the question of the veto and improving peace operations through improved worked methods (see Box 16).

Box 16: Improving the working methods of the Security Council

- Where there are reasonable grounds to justify it, members should be requested to defend their 'no' votes publicly in the Security Council.
- Permanent members should be given the option of casting a 'dissenting vote' that does not rise to the level of a veto and therefore does not block passage of a resolution.
- The Council should ensure sufficient resources and political support to new peace operations where there are potential risks of war crimes.
- For each peace operation a 'Group of Friends' should be constituted, States that can help bring political and diplomatic pressure to bear on the situation.
- The Council must consult troop and police contributing countries whenever there are problems and address their concerns.
- It should undertake a rolling analysis of those terrorist, criminal and extremist elements that are capable of influencing the context of peace operations.

Finally, in assessing the current requirements for social, economic and legal supports for peace and security, the Commission favours instituting a formal mechanism of consultation for regular, structured discussions between the Security Council and representatives of civil society, business and municipalities. After all, these stakeholders have a demonstrated interest in and make specific contributions to the new dimensions of security (health, protection of civilians, women and children, climate change, natural disasters).

2. A more balanced and focused General Assembly

Joseph Schwartzberg (2013) tells us that the General Assembly owes its legitimacy to being an almost universal body with 99.6 per cent of the world's people. This population has tripled since 1945, but for all this time the voting power in the GA has steadily been skewed to favour relatively minor states including a proliferation of microstates. No fewer than 39 current members have less than a million inhabitants each, and 13 have fewer than 100,000 inhabitants each. In financial terms, 128 members collectively pay less than 1.3 per cent of the total UN budget. If one can be opposed to an 'undemocratic' veto then one should be equally opposed to GA coalitions of the very weak. It has been called the 'immoral egalitarianism' of the 'one-member, one-vote' rule. At present, the three most populous countries (China, India and the United States) have 42 per cent of the world's population but only 1.6 per cent of votes in the General Assembly. The major powers resort to bribery or threats to bend the weak to their demands. Because of these faults, the biggest states have opted to create the G20 where they can discuss economic matters without being hobbled by what they consider to be the noisy, 'marginal' states. A well-designed system of weighted voting would mitigate these defects. The aim, as at the beginning of the UN, should be to combine power with principle.

The three basic principles for the weighted vote of each member would be: 1) the democratic principle in which population is the determining factor; 2) economic capacity represented by contributions to the UN budget; and 3) the sovereign equality principle whereby each state is treated equally. The three components of the vote would be combined in a simple formula as if they were of equal relevance (Schwartzberg 2013: 21-26). Over time, say, every ten years, a neutral agency would adjust these weights according to changed conditions. The aim is that states might start listening to each other. Rather than having weak and poor states pass a plethora of meaningless resolutions that destroy the reputation of the GA and are largely ignored by the rich and powerful, debates could become more consequential.

Once the voting power within the General Assembly is more balanced, one could proceed to making its operations more focused. Because global problems require global solutions, Schwartzberg argues that the time has come to give the GA limited capacity to pass legally binding resolutions (in areas not being considered by the Security Council). In matters of a worldwide nature that cannot be addressed at the regional or national levels, the GA should be authorized to legislate binding international law when there is a two-thirds majority that includes 50 per cent of the total world population. Some issues might require a supermajority of 75 per cent of the weighted votes.

3. An Economic, Social and Environmental Council

This book has discussed some of the reasons why analysts have been decrying ECOSOC as the weak sister among the UN's principal organs since at least the 1980s. The UN's founders intended for it to coordinate the economic and social work of the UN system with its specialized agencies and other bodies. Yet they gave the agencies their own governing arrangements; set the Bretton Woods financial institutions on an autonomous path; provided ECOSOC and the General Assembly with overlapping mandates; and failed to give ECOSOC a distinctive profile. From there, everything went downhill. Critics say it is too large for high-level consultations and flexible decision-making, but not large enough to perform credibly as a plenary body. Heads of state, foreign secretaries and finance and trade ministers prefer the smaller, shorter and more focused meetings of the World Bank and IMF. They find ECOSOC to be incapable of dealing with crises, unable to exercise any significant influence over the specialized agencies, and thus only attracting low level delegates to endless debates and little apparent action.

Over the years, there have been a plethora of proposed reforms from different groups. Fearing hang-ups with structural reforms, some observers have limited themselves to suggesting short-term process changes. However, showing the weight of discontent with ECOSOC, structural transformations have been proposed by many groups such as: UBUNTU (World Forum of Civil Society Networks), the Commission on Global Governance, Reimagining the Future, the United Nations Association of the USA, the South Commission and the World Commission on Environment and Development.

The major suggestion coming from these groups is that ECOSOC be transformed to a Social and Economic Security Council or an Economic, Social and Environmental Council (ESEC), with powers and methods parallel to those of the Security Council (without P5 vetoes). Its policy proposals would be transferred back to the GA for debate and majority approval. As with the original intentions of the Charter, the new ESEC would have effective control and coordination over all agencies, financial institutions and multilateral groups in the UN system in the spheres of economics, social development and the environment. The Second and Third Committees of the General Assembly (dealing with economic and financial issues; and social, humanitarian and cultural issues, respectively) would be wound up and their activities transferred to the new ESEC. The UN Conference on Trade and Development (UNCTAD) and the UN Industrial Development Organization (UNIDO) would be closed down. The votes in the World Bank and the IMF would be more equitably distributed. To govern the new council, a ministerial board of some 25 governments could be created along with an advisory commission. Alternatively, the General Committee of the General Assembly could be the leader of ECOSOC. The governing bodies of the major development agencies would be combined into one executive committee.

The Commission on Peace, Justice and Governance outlined an alternative idea to strengthen the United Nation's role in the field of economics without completely redesigning ECOSOC. It proposed transforming the G20 into the G20+. The term 'co-optation' is not used, but this is the essence of the proposal to institutionalize the G20 and strengthen its coordination with the UN, the World Bank, IMF, WTO, ILO and regional organizations. The proposed G20+ would meet every two years at the UN. The UN would furnish a secretariat, a liaison mechanism, a UN deputy secretary-general, and a technical body of experts to frame its activities. The details are shrewd and complex, but this appears to be a subtle manner to bring the G20 within the UN—which is indeed a necessity.

4. A reconfigured Human Rights Council

In Chapter 4 we discussed how the UN has achieved far greater success in developing and promoting human rights than it has in protecting them, and how the politicization of UN human rights bodies, particularly the Human Rights Council, is to blame for this. We also looked at why it may be unlikely that we will see a complete overhaul of the flawed Human Rights Council any time soon, for a host of reasons including the time and resources involved and the optics of another major reform so soon after the 2006 effort.

Box 17: Ideas for reforming the Human Rights Council

- Representation: Governments could remain members but the representatives they select should be judges or academics with human rights expertise. Membership could also be expanded to include independent experts in addition to government representatives.
- Status within UN: The Council could eventually be made a principal UN organ, rather than a subsidiary organ of the General Assembly, though doing so at this time may only elevate its politicization.
- Prevention: Strategies that emphasize preventing conflict and violence that lead to human rights abuses should be pursued.
- Protection: A provision on implementing the Responsibility to Protect could be added to the Council's mandate.
- Universal Periodic Review: The UPR process could integrate a procedure for dealing with violators, to ensure that dialogue and cooperation leads to action.
- NGOs: A more formal institutional framework around the relationship of NGOs to the Council would be beneficial. The consultative status that NGOs enjoy with ECOSOC would be a model to follow.

But that does not mean we cannot make certain changes that would have a measurable impact on the Human Rights Council's work. In doing so, we should focus on what is realistic and achievable. Ramcharan (2011) outlines a number of actionable ideas that could help make the body more fair, impartial and effective (see Box 17). These vary in level of ambition.

Reforming the Human Rights Council will not be straightforward—especially if the reform process of the Commission on Human Rights is any indication—but in the long run, failing to even try will have devastating consequences.

5. *Improved staffing and management practices*

There is a general consensus among experts that the UN's approach to hiring and managing the international civil service needs fixing.

One of the chief criticisms of the Secretariat relates to the politicized approach to hiring, particularly when it comes to top appointments. Since it was launched in 2014, the 1 for 7 Billion campaign has made appeals for greater transparency regarding top UN appointments, and an end to the current monopoly over the decisions. It explains how permanent Security Council members have dominated the selection process for secretaries-general, often supporting candidates in exchange for promises to reserve senior posts for their own nationals. Multiple examples are provided, for instance how since 1997 the Department of Peacekeeping Operations has been led by four successive nationals of France, and how five successive US nationals headed the Department of Management from 1992-2007 (since 2007, Americans have led the Department of Political Affairs). There are similar cases of posts held by UK, Russian and Chinese nationals for multiple terms. This practice thus prevents nationals from other countries from holding these positions. 1 for 7 Billion argues that the selection process should be based exclusively on merit, as stipulated in the UN Charter, so that the secretary-general can recruit a strong leadership team from all the world's regions (1 for 7 Billion 2016).

The Commission on Global Security, Justice and Governance made related calls, stating that, through the General Assembly, member states politicize hiring at all levels by micromanaging the budget. As well, despite having some influence on the selection process, the Secretary-General can neither appoint nor let go the heads of UN agencies, programs, and funds. The Commission highlighted a need for the Secretary-General to have greater discretion to manage the Secretariat. For the appointment of under-secretaries-general and assistant secretaries-general, it proposes that member states continue to approve the selections, but that the Secretary-General be presented with an array of candidates from which to choose (2015: 93).

A second issue increasingly in the spotlight relates to management practices. In former Australian Prime Minister Kevin Rudd's recent report, he calls for "deep reforms of the UN management system", arguing that the organization relies on "rigid staffing" and that its "excessively hierarchical structure is a legacy from an earlier age" (2016: 21,35). He draws attention to some of the main challenges, from the inability of managers to move employees either within or between agencies, to the length of time involved in hiring people (up to 12 months) and the difficulty of firing people. He also disapproves of what he refers to as the "demise of a permanent, professional, international public service", whereby the ability of long-standing and highly-experienced UN staff to rise to senior management positions is being weakened by an increase in external, political appointments. He makes a strong case for a flatter, flexible, effective, and cross-disciplinary structure that can better respond to complex challenges.

Finally, Rudd claims that more of the Secretariat's staff should be in the field, rather than at headquarters (at present they are roughly equally divided). This would help shift the UN's work from report writing to executing its mandate on the ground. At the same time he states that the opportunities for advancement are disproportionately at headquarters, and that deserving field staff should be encouraged, rewarded and promoted (ibid: 33). Weiss (2009) has echoed these sentiments, calling for an end to the tendency for promotions to result from work and contacts in pleasant headquarter settings.

6. Autonomous emergency services for the UN

It is unlikely that reformed structures alone will be enough to help the United Nations to fulfil its mandate for global protection and development. The organization will also require additional resources to give it the autonomy to carry out its work. This proposal will look at a suggestion that has come from multiple experts for giving the UN its own emergency, rapid reaction peace force, while the next will cover ideas for independent sources of income.

One of the leading proponents of a United Nations Emergency Peace Service (UNEPS), Peter Langille (2015), has pointed out that UN peacekeepers, over the years, have helped improve conditions in 69 armed conflicts worldwide. The chief problem is that it currently takes 6-12 months for the UN to mount a peace operation—as opposed to the seven days it took to deploy forces to the first UN peacekeeping in the Suez in 1956. In addition, Western countries with their advanced militaries are now only contributing a minimal number of the 120,000 troops the UN has in the field. In part because of this slow reaction, the UN is now spending $8.2 billion annually on peacekeeping, but only after conflicts have spread, thousands have died and countries have been destroyed.

Creating a UNEPS would help prevent the spread of conflict along with the ensuing mass atrocities and huge costs. Its principal characteristics would be:

- a permanent standing, integrated UN formation;
- highly trained and well-equipped;
- ready for immediate deployment by the Security Council;
- composed of soldiers, police and civilian experts ('multidimensional');
- capable of diverse assignments (e.g., security, environmental and health crises);
- 13,000 to 15,000 professional volunteers;
- equitable regional and gender representation; and
- a first responder to cover the initial six months until member states can deploy.

The central aim of UNEPS would be to deter aggression and its spread. There would be sufficient military forces and police to restore and maintain order and civilian teams to provide essential services. Its approximate start-up costs of $3 billion and recurring costs of $1.5 billion annually, while significant, are trifling in comparison to the $13.6 trillion in annual military expenditures globally (Global Peace Index). A very similar proposal has been presented in great detail by Robert Johansen in "A United Nations Emergency Peace Service: To Prevent Genocide and Crimes Against Humanity".

7. Financing the UN

Over the years, UN proponents have put forth a whole series of ideas for finding innovative, alternative sources of funding for the organization. The basic problem is that the regular assessments of member states (even when they are paid) have never provided a sufficient budget to finance the UN's multitude of operations. When these are supplemented by voluntary contributions from states, they are still insufficient and tend to reflect the priorities of the particular donor. They have been called the 'UN à la carte'. So, there has been an ongoing search for additional and independent financial resources for the UN. There is no lack of ingenuity in proposals, which have included imposing levies (a sort of international tax) on air and sea travel, arms sales, transnational movements of currencies, international trade, the production of polluting materials, and production from the global commons such as mining of sea nodules—even an annual UN lottery has been suggested. The trick is to keep it international, find huge areas of untaxed transactions, and place the levy low so that it will not cause a backlash. A good example is the air travel tax that France introduced in 2005 to finance Unitaid, which was implemented by nine countries.

Yet none of these relatively simple and ingenious ideas has ever been implemented on a global scale. Many critics believe that member states have not given the UN permission to impose such levies because they do not want the organization to have its own independent sources of revenue. Rather, they wish to retain full control. It is this attitude on the part of governments that must be one of the major targets of a reform movement.

This latter consideration caused Joseph Schwartzberg to propose that the easiest path would simply be for the UN to return to its original financial well in a more astute manner. He proposes scrapping the present complicated and contentious system used to calculate member state assessments, and replacing it by one wherein all states are assessed at a "very small, affordable and equal percentage" (say 0.1 per cent initially) of their respective gross national incomes (GNI). He calculates that if such a GNI assessment had been in place in 2010, it would have generated $58.65 billion—more than twice the total current spending for the entire UN system (2013: 201-24).

Tax evasion is another issue that harms national budgets, and thus the UN's budget. In his book *Options for Strengthening Global Tax Governance,* Wolfgang Obenland calls on the UN to create new institutions for a platform for tax collaboration. He claims the world is losing hundreds of billions in tax revenues annually because of a lack of international cooperation on tax issues which permits rich individuals and corporations to evade or avoid taxes in offshore tax havens or to demand preferential treatment in their host countries.

8. Principles and criteria for the Responsibility to Protect

It is time to complete what the United Nations neglected when it adopted the resolution on the Responsibility to Protect (R2P) at the UN Summit in 2005. In itself, it was one of the most significant steps to place some limits on the abuse of national sovereignty. But the resolution omitted two of the most important elements of the report of the International Commission on Intervention and State Sovereignty, which had formulated the concept of R2P. These were the 'Principles for Military Intervention' that formed the criteria for when the Security Council needed to act, and, even more alarmingly, the whole chapter on 'the Responsibility to Prevent' which dealt with early warning, analysis of root causes, and the techniques of prevention.

Without clear principles for intervention, the UN lacked the key instruments for deciding when to put R2P into action. Some wicked tongues claimed this was exactly the intention of some of the P5. If this was the case, it backfired. When the Security Council authorized the NATO intervention in Libya, the principles of 'right intention' and 'proportional means' and the operational 'principle of limitations' were not on hand to guide the resolution. So, NATO went on to overthrow the government of Libya rather than just halting or averting human suffering. As we have discussed, this has been the basis of Russia and China vetoing UN intervention in Syria with the results we know.

The Commission put forth six principles that should be respected before the UN would decide on military intervention in the name of protecting civilian populations:

- The 'just cause threshold' stated that there had to be actual or apprehended large scale loss of life or ethnic cleansing. Human rights violations, the overthrow of democracy, or the desire to rescue one's nationals were not sufficient cause.
- The 'right intention' principle said the intervention must be to avert human suffering which could best be assured by 'multilateral operations' supported by regional opinion and the victims concerned.
- The 'last resort' principle stipulated that every form of negotiation and non-military forms of arm-twisting had to have been exhausted.
- The principle of 'proportional means' asserted that the scale, duration and intensity of the intervention has to be the minimum necessary to achieve the human rights objectives.
- The principle of 'reasonable prospects' insisted there has to be reasonable chances of success and that action will not be worse than inaction.
- The principle of 'right authority' stipulates that the Security Council is the appropriate body for authorizing interventions, but it should act promptly. In addition, the Permanent Five should not apply their veto power except when their vital state interests are involved. If the Security Council fails to act in a reasonable time, an alternative option would be for the General Assembly to consider the matter in an Emergency Special Session under the 'Uniting for Peace' procedure, or a regional organization might take action.

In addition to these R2P principles for military intervention, the Commission also proposed 'operational principles' including clear objectives, unity of command, limitations in the application of force ("for the protection of the population, not for defeat of the state"), adherence to international law, and coordination with humanitarian organizations.

It is high time the UN gave due consideration to these criteria and principles for the use of R2P.

9. The dispersion and control of global power

Most experts agree that providing the United Nations with greater authority is a necessity. Thomas Weiss has courageously taken the bull by the horns in his recent publications. In his 2009 book, *What's Wrong with the United Nations and How to Fix It,* he closes with the statement, "global government rather than global governance is a necessary part of future analytical perspectives." (232). Latterly, in *Governing the World,* Weiss concludes, "We cannot continue to ignore and rationalize the absence of overarching authority… Humanity collectively is capable of better and more fairly governing the world." (2014a: 101).

Similarly, French thinker Jacques Attali summed this view up well, stating "Neither an empire nor the marketplace will be able to master the immense problems which await the world. For that it will require a world government. This government will take a form fairly close to today's federal regimes. ... Leaving to the national governments the responsibility for assuring the specific rights of each people and the protection of each culture, the global government will be in charge of the general interest of the planet and verifying that each nation respects the rights of each citizen of humanity." (2011: 10).

However, there is a widespread fear of a more authoritative global institution. Since the time of Immanuel Kant, the fear of a global leviathan has been one of the main arguments against giving enhanced authority to the United Nations or any other international institution. Unfortunately, even cosmopolitans share this fear of big government—even if, aside from this, they are some of the strongest proponents of a reformed international system. It is reflected too in science fiction where we have the forces of the 'Federation' confronting those who want to install an evil and all-powerful oppressor.

One of the most serious warnings came from Michael Barnett and Martha Finnemore in their book *Rules for the World.* Their research focused on international organizations as bureaucracies. They point out that we have known ever since the work of the German sociologist, Max Weber, that bureaucracy is a distinctive social form with its own internal logic that generates specific behavioural tendencies which might be good or bad.

According to the authors, bureaucracies can govern complex situations because of their rules-based, hierarchical, continuous, impersonal, and expert nature. They control access to knowledge and their rational process makes them both proficient and efficient. Moreover, rules shape their activities, understandings, identity, and practices, along with how bureaucrats see the world and perceive social problems. Bureaucrats often make rules that prescribe the behaviour of others. When we think about the activities of the UN and the European Commission in this light, we can see why there has been growing reaction against often inappropriate rules applied by distant, impersonal, so-called experts who are unaware of local conditions. This is, in large part, driving the rise of populism.

The analysis by Barnett and Finnemore shows that there is a danger lurking in the nearly 300 international organizations that manage much of the world's relationships. These organizations are lauded for advancing liberal goals such as human rights and economic growth, but behind this liberal façade is the reality that they do so using undemocratic procedures. They note how Weber recognized that "a bureaucratic world had its own perils, producing increasingly powerful and autonomous bureaucrats who could be 'spiritless' and driven by rules, who could apply those rules in ways that harmed the people whom they were expected to serve." (2004: 172-73).

We must take these warnings to heart as we contemplate ever-more powerful international organizations. There will be bureaucracies. Yet the well-founded concerns some have of a 'world government' can be addressed by designing transformed global institutions based on the diffusion and control of power. As Trent began to elaborate in his *Modernizing the United Nations System* (2007: 237-40, 256-8), the best way to do this is by applying what democracies have learnt about diffusing and controlling power during the past two hundred years. The techniques of federalism, subsidiarity, checks and balances, the division of powers, constitutionally guaranteed freedoms, rights and equality, liberalism, the rule of law, transparency and participation all help to decentralize power. To these can be added the more specific freedoms of speech, thought, association and the freedom of the press. While at first glance it may not appear so, the rising inequality between and within countries also has a tendency to reinforce established power. The wealthy often use their money to influence the political elite to develop policies that reinforce their wealth—creating a vicious circle. The control and dispersion of power must include the struggle against inequality.

Democracy itself is at the core of the dispersal of power. Many associate democracy with electoral techniques, but it is far more complex than that. There is a long list of attributes often considered as the defining properties of democracy: free, fair and frequent elections, competition, participation, contestation, civil liberties, rights, freedom of expression, information and association, rule of law, an effective state, accountability, equality, inclusive citizenship, individual and minority rights, checks and balances, constitutional protection, and an active civil society (Geissel et al, 2016). Taken together, these properties ensure the circulation, distribution, division and control of power, a key objective of democracy. Two centuries ago, few gave the nascent democracies much chance of persisting but because of the control of power we have come a long way. These techniques must be replicated in any proposals for the reform of global institutions.

Another concept we may briefly expand upon is world federalism. Federalism is a mechanism for creating rules and norms for the distribution of jurisdictions and for a continuing, principled struggle for power. Under federalism, each political unit maintains its own 'sovereign' responsibilities and authorities. In functioning federations with a constitutional enforcement and multiple political parties, there is no concentration of power. It is a fundamental technique for ensuring that the 'centre' does not accumulate too much 'authority'. It is also what has allowed vast territories such as Canada and the United States to have one central government along with a great dispersal of power in the provinces/territories or states. Thus, world federalism would promote a continuing balancing of power between states and a UN with more authority. So, we can assume that if the UN had small but autonomous emergency peace forces and sources of funding, the member states would still have their national military and police forces along with their own legislatures, judiciaries, public services and everything else that goes to make sovereign nation-states.

It should be added that so-called federalism is also the governing authority in countries such as Russia which are not exactly shining models of democracy and freedom. So, we must understand that federalism is a necessary technique for the dispersion of power but by no means a sufficient one for ensuring the decentralization and control of authority.

Worrying about the techniques of global democracy and world federalism may not appear to be of immediate concern, but considering the multiple techniques for the control and distribution of power in international organizations with more decision-making authority needs to be a priority.

Sequencing reform proposals: where to start

This list of possible transformations of the UN leads immediately to the question: where to start? The next section, which will conclude this book, explores a possible path to mobilizing public and political support for reform so it is placed on the international agenda. Before getting to this, it is necessary to consider how to begin to sequence reform proposals.

As we have said, it is not our intention to present a comprehensive program or step-by-step plan for reform. Rather, we wanted to demonstrate to the reader the extent of thinking that has already gone into UN reform and offer a panoply of proposals to work from. There are many more that have come from scholars, civil society and other UN experts. To sort or rank these issues is no small task. Developing a methodological approach is helpful. Some of the questions we need to ask when considering how to prioritize are: How urgently is the reform needed? How large is it in scale and scope? How easily could it be achieved? What would the cost be? How much time might it take? Is there/would there be political will? Is there/would there be public support? How developed are the proposals? Is there consensus among experts on what needs to be done? Is there a strong champion behind it?

Joseph Schwartzberg (2013) gives considerable thought to the sequencing of UN reforms. He suggests that some changes are easier to get accepted, and that starting with these may open the door to further reforms. His preference would be to begin with: improving UN funding via a new assessment system; regaining legitimacy through weighted voting in all the UN organs (i.e., including population and the economic contributions of states in their voting power rather than just one-state-one-vote); creating a Security Council that is universally representative with weighted regional voting and no veto; and establishing a standing, all volunteer UN peace force.

Few disagree that the UN must have its own sources of revenue, although many would prefer this to come from some form of taxation. Many also accept the need for some form of emergency peace force. Still, to get these two resources, the organization must have legitimacy. This is why weighted voting is such an important concept. The European Union has used weighted voting and it appears to work quite well. In the context of global institutions, it could help address the issue of large countries fleeing the cacophony of the UN towards the G7 and G20, in part to have their voices heard for their just value.

Four steps toward the renaissance of the United Nations

We have come to the conclusion that significant groundwork needs to be done before reforms will get under way. The whole issue of renewing the UN must be placed on the international agenda. This will take considerable leadership, education and communication. At the same time, overcoming established interests and natural tendencies for maintaining the status quo will require immense mobilization of popular support to create political will. In all likelihood, neither of these will be achieved without the efforts of a committed and sustained movement pushing for change in this direction. This final section explores how we can bring about a civil society-led UN renaissance movement, and how strategic campaigning and advocacy can garner the public support and political will required for transformative change.

1. Mapping actors and interests

A useful first step in building a successful movement for reform, one that garners enough popular support to lead to political action, is having a deep understanding of the players involved. This is as true for allies as it is for opponents.

Let's begin by identifying potential allies to help spot opportunities for coalition building. A first step is seeking out civil society organizations that advocate for more effective global governance and share a common vision for a fairer and more legitimate UN. There are also a number of groupings of states that have voiced their concerns about the status quo and have called for reforms at the UN. Some of these governments may be willing to join efforts to collectively push for action. There are also allies within the UN and other international organizations who would like to see a more effective global institution. The core of change will come from a partnership of NGOs and like-minded states plus reformers in the UN.

Not all those identified as allies will be focused on the same issue areas, nor will they necessarily agree on how to fix some of the problems. Issue-specific groups or committees can be formed to deal with this, as was done with the NGO Coalition for an International Criminal Court, discussed in Box 18.

Of course, not everyone favours a rational and progressive path to more workable global institutions. The most obvious opposition has come from member states themselves, particularly the most powerful ones. The recent wave of right-wing populist nationalism spreading across the West poses an additional threat to attempts at reform, as anti-globalism sentiment is paired with isolationist policies, trade barriers, and restrictions on the movement of people. Such politicians are responding to the understandable frustration that many have felt as a result of the gains from globalization not being equitably shared, and from the challenges that have come with greater regional and global integration. Yet rather than working to improve global institutions to better manage the harmful consequences of living in a globalized world, they are proposing to reverse the positive achievements of the past decades, including gains made on climate change policies, trade, regionalism and multilateralism, diplomacy, efforts to improve taxation and environmental regulation, humanitarianism, multiculturalism, arms reductions and peace and security.

Potential opposition could also come from all those who benefit from international conflict, inequality and general disarray. Among them are the wealthiest one per cent (who collectively control over fifty per cent of the world's capital), who may not support a more regulated international regime that might, for example, combat offshore tax havens. There are also those who benefit economically from war and world military spending, which in 2016 was estimated at $1.7 trillion. And of course there are the many perpetrators of conflict and war.

Not all sets of actors will have clearly identifiable interests or roles. The media (which admittedly is a broad term that reflects a wide diversity of organizations, from CNN to DemocracyNow! to Breitbart News) has played different roles at different times. On the one hand, there was a great deal of balanced, high quality reporting in the mainstream media around the time of the UN's 70th anniversary that recognized the organization's many achievements while also pointing to a need for change. At the same time, the media has often painted the UN in a negative light, as was the case in late 2016 when it failed to report on a successful example of countries uniting against Security Council inaction in Syria, opting instead to lambaste it over appointing Wonder Woman as honorary ambassador. Given the fairly direct link between media coverage and public opinion, this example may help explain why we have a relatively ill-informed and ambivalent public.

There are additional actors and interests that should be mapped out too, many of which may not be clear allies or opponents. These include various parts of the UN system itself, regional groupings, faith-based organizations, multinational corporations and others that have been explored throughout this book.

2. Form smart coalitions of allies

For many of the more substantial reforms ideas to materialize, a coalition, or perhaps multiple coalitions, will likely need to be formed to drive a wider movement. Among the attributes of these 'smart coalitions' comprising NGOs and some governments are: ideas, leadership, expertise, skilful negotiations, mobilization of networks and resources, concrete agendas, targets and indicators, and tools to measure progress and respond to setbacks.

In terms of personnel, they will require NGO experts, international practitioners, communicators, academics, retired politicians and ideally some representatives of willing governments. Often, complex reforms must be organized into manageable, issue-specific areas that can be overseen by actors with specific expertise.

It is useful to learn from past examples of successful coalitions, such as the Coalition for an International Criminal Court, the International Coalition for R2P, the International Campaign to Ban Landmines, and 1 for 7 Billion, all of which were mobilized by the World Federalist Movement. These campaigns came along when conditions in the General Assembly opened the door to creating momentum for the specific reform. NGOs and governments made use of each other's relative advantages. NGOs applied their expertise, their ability to inform the media and frame the discourse, and their means for embarrassing dissenting governments through naming-and-shaming campaigns. Friendly governments used their money and resources to manage negotiations and decision-making. Campaigns were based on a strong and simple normative message. Instead of meeting opposition governments head-on (even the P5), the coalitions moved around them through the support of a strong majority of states. The Coalition for an International Criminal Court is explored in greater detail in Box 18.

This idea is not new. The report by the Commission on Security, Justice and Governance (which we have analyzed at length in this chapter) called for a World Conference on Global Institutions that could "serve as a rallying point for smart coalitions and simultaneously generate political momentum for multiple, urgent global reforms" (109-110). The Commission proposes that the Conference take place in 2020 to mark the UN's 75th anniversary, and that it be the culmination of a three-year multilateral negotiation process on global institutional reform. It highlighted the need to include diverse voices, including those at the most local level and those of under-represented groups. A number of scholars have also called for the creation of NGO coalitions for UN reform, including Trent in his 2007 book *Modernizing the United Nations System.* And indeed, a small number of NGOs are already working toward a 2020 UN reform congress.

Box 18: An NGO coalition that made history

The Coalition for the International Criminal Court (CICC) started in 1995 when 25 civil society organizations joined together to advocate for a permanent international criminal court. By 1997, the Coalition had grown to 450 organizations. After three and a half years of intense advocacy and deep collaboration among NGOs and between NGOs, governments and the UN Secretariat, governments held a diplomatic conference in Rome and 120 countries adopted the Rome Statute that established the ICC. The Coalition's role was enormous. The information-sharing, legal analysis and advocacy that it undertook prior to and during the conference is widely seen as having shaped the outcome. The Coalition is credited with a number of achievements, namely the independent nature of the Court and its prosecutor, strong victim and witness protection, and the inclusion of gender crimes.

Coordinating the 200+ NGOs that attended the conference and achieving the results they did was a major feat. The Coalition included a steering committee of a dozen NGOs and regional caucuses that represented all the world's regions. Thematic caucuses were formed to delve into specific issues. These were: Women's Initiative for Gender Justice, Victims' Rights Working Group, Faith-Based Caucus, Universal Jurisdiction Caucus, Children's Caucus, and Peace Caucus. The World Federalist Movement–Institute for Global Policy (WFM–IGP) and its Executive Director, William R. Pace, served as Secretariat for the entire network.

Over 20 years later, the Coalition remains as active as ever. Its recent efforts in the fight for international justice have focused on encouraging African countries to stay with the ICC, restraining the Security Council veto (which prevented the investigation of crimes in Syria) and trying to halt government attempts to undermine the Court.

Source: Coalition for the ICC website

3. Marketing the UN and its achievements to build public support

A main task of a smart coalition would be to generate public support for more authoritative global institutions through an effective marketing campaign. Those in other fields and industries seem to understand the importance of marketing far better than those desiring UN reform. Consider the entrepreneurs who often spend more time on marketing than they do on inventing. Or the athletes who work as hard on their game plans as they do on muscle building. Or the movie moguls who put as much effort into attracting the public as they do in producing films. Those seeking reforms need to convey the UN's importance as well as its numerous achievements to an audience that remains unconvinced that better global governance is even necessary. This will take considerable leadership, education and communication. It will also take outside specialists from diverse disciplines—like strategists, communicators, educators, psychologists, behavioural economists, marketers, and mobilizers.

Throughout this book we have observed our collective incapacity to develop policies and take actions to adequately deal with the challenges that go beyond the capacities of any single state. We explored how the UN needs new institutional capacities to fill this void, and how a first step in this direction is to continue efforts to harness sovereignty. The question is, how precisely do we lead citizens to look favourably on more UN authority?

Some useful insights were provided by Matthias Ecker-Ehrhardt in his article "Why do citizens want the UN to decide?". He studied the fifth wave of the World Values Survey and drew several conclusions about public attitudes toward giving more decisional authority to the UN. First, he found that, in general, public support for UN authority is strongly linked to individuals believing that many problems we face are of a global scope and that nation-states are unable to handle them on their own. A second finding is that citizens of powerful nations view UN authority more favourably because their power base allows them to establish international institutional arrangements that preserve their interests. Finally, he found that the social legitimacy of world institutions is already in short supply. Global governance 'architects' or 'entrepreneurs'—those pushing for reform—should be aware that any attempt to simply 'upload' more authority to existing institutions is likely to lead to further backlash. Ecker-Ehrhardt concluded that institutional inequality and skewed distribution of power must be convincingly addressed before effective global institutions will be widely accepted.

The takeaway from this research is that the more people think global challenges surpass the capacities of states, the more they will support global authorities—except when they think present world institutions are skewed in the favour of major powers or special interests, in which case they will demand institutional reform that spreads power more equitably. Marketing and communications efforts must address these lessons.

Of course, engaging the public should not be the sole responsibility of a civil society-led coalition for reform. The UN itself needs to invest more time and energy in its public relations. This observation was made recently by Kevin Rudd, who recommended that the UN appoint a chief communications officer to "overhaul the UN's communications structure and strategy in order to effectively communicate its message to member states, the general public, the media, and the rest of the UN system" (2016: 62). His rationale is precisely what we have argued, "The UN has a good story to tell, but it is not telling it effectively." He proposed that the UN develop a new communications strategy that makes use of all media platforms in multiple languages, and uses plain language rather than "UN dialect, which is incomprehensible to the rest of the world." While it is made clear that this would not be a substitute for the individual communications efforts of UN agencies, Rudd stressed the need for a UN-wide approach to enhancing the integrity of its brand.

4. Transforming public support into political action

Can we assume that an effective social movement and a corresponding shift in public opinion will lead to political will for change? The short answer is yes. A wealth of research has been produced over the past decades on the impact of public opinion on public policy, and the evidence is compelling. In his book *How Change Happens,* Duncan Green, author and Head of Research at Oxfam, explores how activists have succeeded in achieving norm change (2016: 48-56). While acknowledging that on rare occasions governments have been the source of new norms, he explains how many core features of the state, such as social protection, education and healthcare, were formulated by activists before being taken up by the state. This was similarly the case with securing various group rights, including women's rights, children's rights, disabled people's rights and gay rights. The typical trajectory is that activists gain public support, and politicians respond to voters' desires by implementing change.

In their piece "When the pillars fall: how social movements can win more victories like same-sex marriage", Mark and Paul Engler (2014) describe how the fight for marriage equality in the US was one where the consensus view held by the public changed, for a host of reasons, and politicians and legal rulings responded. "The change has come about through a mass withdrawal of cooperation from a past order based on prejudice. It could be felt well before it was written into law, and well before it was acknowledged by those leaders now struggling to show that they have 'evolved'." As recently as 1990, 75 per cent of Americans saw homosexuality as immoral. Politicians knew that expressing support for same-sex marriage could end their career. In 1996, the U.S. Senate passed the *Defense of Marriage Act,* which narrowly defined marriage and denied federal benefits to same-sex couples, by an overwhelming majority. But the movement slowly chipped away at the "pillars of support", the institutions of society that legitimized the status quo. In this case, denying equal rights to same-sex couples was a system propped up by the churches, the media, the business community, the military, the educational system, the courts, and so on.

Gains were made on a range of fronts and public support for same-sex marriage rose steadily until it reached a tipping point—in 2011, polls showed it to be more than 50 per cent for the first time in history. The tide of public opinion had turned, and legal and political victories came in rapid succession. In 2012, President Obama stated that he had changed his position on the issue, as did Bill Clinton who had led the *Defense of Marriage Act* just a decade and a half earlier. In a single week in April 2013 six U.S. Senators came out in support for marriage equality. This example presents an important lesson for other social movements: "Rather than being based on calculating realism—a shrewd assessment of what was attainable in the current political climate—the drive for marriage equality drew on a transformational vision." (Engler and Engler, 2014).

Of course, this case is from the US, which has strong democratic institutions. To what extent does the assumption that public opinion leads to political change hold in places with undemocratic regimes? After all, demands are filtered through domestic political institutions and the sensitivity of political elites to the demands of voters varies greatly. Yet the "pillars of support" notion is every bit as applicable. If civil servants, the military, merchants and all others effectively propping up a regime were to suddenly refuse to cooperate, they could bring down even the most authoritarian dictatorship. By removing enough pillars, the temple will topple and the tyrant will tumble (ibid).

It should be clear from this example and others explored in this book that social movements matter. In many cases, they are the single most important factor leading to change. Take for example the research conducted by Laurel Weldon and Mala Htun on what factors drive change in government policies on violence against women around the globe, which Green presents in his book (2016: 55-56). Gathering data from 70 countries over four decades on various forms of state action (legal and administrative reforms, prevention measures, training, etc.) and other factors such as women legislators, level of economic development, political regime. They concluded that, when all else is equal, it was the presence of strong feminist movements that made the single largest impact on whether a country had comprehensive policies addressing violence against women or not. Public opinion and political pressure can and do lead to political action.

To summarize, we have now seen from domestic and international politics that creating significant political change has a number of components. Informed citizens need to recognize a massive public problem, in this case that existing international organizations do not have the capacity to surmount global problems. Activists need to rally around a transformational vision, likely in partnership with politicians and other allies. A movement for reform needs to be launched—ideally one that seeks to undermine the pillars of support for maintaining the status quo. Broad public support needs to be gained, in order to influence the decision-making of elites.

Concluding remarks

History suggests that a reform movement will most likely start when a small number of like-minded states and numerous civil society organizations with strong leadership and communications skills can mobilize widespread and sustained support for a UN with adequate authority. This should be an immediate focus of activists concerned with our current collective inability to govern the world.

It is worth reminding ourselves that if nationalist and isolationist politics continue to gain traction, all these potential reforms may be cast aside—for the moment. If they are, they will come back into their own as ever more citizens recognize that the renaissance of world institutions is required to deal with global issues. It may also result in their return to the spotlight, with the reform agenda being seen as more urgent than ever. The UN and the League were founded both on cumulative historical developments and on the impetus coming from the scourge of world wars. But with modern weapons, we likely could not survive another world clash. We must hope that the fear of global catastrophes will force world leaders to choose reform over conflict or chaos. The crisis of multilateralism may just shed enough light on what we risk losing to bring the doubters and believers together to revitalize the UN.

> *"You may never know what results come of your actions but if you do nothing there will be no results"* Mahatma Gandhi

Bibliography

1 for 7 Billion (2016). "Campaign Calls for Transparency and End To Monopoly On Top UN Appointments". Accessed April 7, 2017. http://www.1for7billion.org/news/2016/6/13/campaign-calls-for-transparency-and-end-to-monopoly-on-top-un-appointments.

Adams, Barbara and Karen Judd (2016). *Reinventing Development: Reforming the UN for People and Planet,* Rosa Luxemburg Stiftung New York Office.

A Fair Globalization: Creating Opportunities for All (2004). Report of the Commission on the Social Dimensions of Globalization, Geneva, International Labour Organization.

Amnesty International (2016). "World Leaders have Shirked Responsibility on Refugee Crisis". Accessed April 7, 2017. https://www.amnesty.org/en/press-releases/2016/09/world-leaders-have-shirked-responsibility-on-refugee-crisis/.

Amnesty International (2017). "Syria: Secret campaign of mass hangings and extermination at Saydnaya Prison". Accessed April 7, 2017. https://www.amnesty.org/en/latest/news/2017/02/syria-investigation-uncovers-governments-secret-campaign-of-mass-hangings-and-extermination-at-saydnaya-prison/.

Annan, Kofi (2005). *In Larger Freedom: Toward Development, Security, and Human Rights, Report of the Secretary-General.* Accessed April 7, 2017. http://www.un.org/en/ga/search/view_doc.asp?symbol=A/59/2005.

Archer, C. (2001). *International Organizations* (3rd ed.), London, Routledge.

Attali, Jacques (2011). *Demain, qui gouvernera le monde?* Paris, Fayard.

Axworthy, Lloyd (2003). *Navigating a New World: Canada's Global Future,* Toronto, Alfred A. Knopf.

Barnett, Chance (2015). "Trends Show Crowdfunding To Surpass VC In 2016". Forbes. Accessed April 7, 2017. http://www.forbes.com/sites/chancebarnett/2015/06/09/trends-show-crowdfunding-to-surpass-vc-in-2016/#5cabae18444b.

Barrnett, Michael and Martha Finnemore (2004). *Rules for the World: International Organizations in Global Politics,* Ithica, Cornell University Press.

Basic Facts about the United Nations (2014) New York, United Nations Department of Public Information.

British Council and SEUK (2015). "Think Global Trade Social: How business with a social purpose can deliver more sustainable development". Accessed April 7, 2017. https://www.britishcouncil.org/sites/default/files/seuk_british_council_think_global_report.pdf.

Browne, Stephen and Thomas G. Weiss, ed. (2014). *Post-2015 UN Development: Making change happen?* Oxon/New York, Routledge.

Cameron, Maxwell A. (2002). "Global Civil Society and the Ottawa Process: Lessons from the movement to ban anti-personnel mines", Andrew Cooper et al. op.cit.

Caron, David (1993). "The Legitimacy of the Collective Authority of the Security Council", *American Journal of International Law.*

Chase-Dunn Christopher & Salvatore J. Babones (2006), *Global Social Change,* Baltimore, The John Hopkins University Press.

Chesterman, Simon (2015). "The Secretary-General We Deserve?", *Global Governance,* 21(4).

Childers, Erskine with Brian Urquhart (1994). *Renewing the United Nations System,* Uppsala, Sweden, the Dag Hammarskjöld Foundation.

Claude, I.L. (1966). *Swords into Ploughshares: The Problems and Progress of International Organizations,* London, University of London Press.

Coalition for the International Criminal Court website. Accessed April 7, 2017. http://www.coalitionfortheicc.org/.

Commission on Global Security, Justice and Governance (2015). *Confronting the Crisis of Global Governance,* Hague Institute for Global Justice and Washington, the Stimson Centre.

Compare Your Country. Official Development Assistance 2015. Accessed April 7, 2017. http://www2.compareyourcountry.org/oda?cr=20001&cr1=oecd&lg=en&page=1.

Cooper, Andrew et al (eds.) (2002). *Enhancing Global Governance: Towards a New Diplomacy?* Tokyo, United Nations University Press.

Corner, Mark (2010). *The Binding of Nations: From European Union to World Union,* Houndmills, U.K., Palgrave Macmillan.

Cumming-Bruce, Nick (2016). "Donald Trump is 'Dangerous' for Global Stability, U.N. Rights Chief Says". New York Times. Accessed April 7, 2017._http://www.nytimes.com/2016/10/13/world/europe/donald-trump-un-human-rights.html?.

Deudney, Daniel (2006). *Bounding Power: Republican Security Theory from the Polis to the Global Village,* Princeton, Princeton University Press.

Dodds, Felix (2015). "Multi-stakeholder partnerships: Making them work for the Post-2015 Development Agenda". Accessed April 7, 2017._http://www.un.org/en/ecosoc/newfunct/pdf15/2015partnerships_background_note.pdf.

Doyle, Michael W. & Nicholas Sambanis (2007). "Peacekeeping Operations" in Weiss & Daws op.cit.

Ecker-Ehrhardt, Matthias (2016). "Why do citizens want the UN to decide? Cosmopolitan ideas, particularism, and global authority", *International Political Science Review,* 37(1).

Economic and Social Council (ECOSOC, 2016). Meetings coverage: Partnership Forum on March 31, 2016. "Sustainable Development Goals Offer Chance to Create Synergies between All Parties, Special Advisor Says at Economic and Social Council Partnership Forum". Accessed April 7, 2017._http://www.un.org/press/en/2016/ecosoc6746.doc.htm.

Engler, Mark and Paul Engler (2014). "When the pillars fall: how social movements can win more victories like same-sex marriage". Waging Nonviolence. Accessed April 7, 2017. http://wagingnonviolence.org/feature/pillars-fall-social-movements-can-win-victories-like-sex-marriage/.

Evans, Gareth (2015). Speech: "Responsibility to Protect: After Libya and Syria". Accessed April 7, 2017._http://www.gevans.org/speeches/speech585.html.

A Fair Globalization: Creating Opportunities for All (2004). Report of the Commission on the Social Dimensions of Globalization, Geneva, International Labour Organization.

Fasulo, Linda (2015). *The Insider's Guide to the UN,* 3rd Edition, Yale University Press.

Freedman, Rosa (2011). *The UN Human Rights Council: A Critique and Early Assessment.* Doctoral thesis, University of London.

Freedman, Rosa (2015). *Failing to Protect: The UN and the Politicization of Human Rights,* New York, Oxford University Press.

Future United Nations Development System (FUNDS, 2014). UN FUNDS 2014 survey. Accessed April 7, 2017._http://futureun.org/media/archive1/surveys/FUNDS2014Surveysummaryresults.pdf.

Future United Nations Development System (FUNDS, 2016). Delivering As One: Could it Help the 2030 SDG Agenda? Accessed April 7, 2017._http://futureun.org/en/Publications-Surveys/Article?newsid=85.

Gaffey, Conor (2016). "Uganda: Museveni Calls ICC 'Useless', Prompts Western Leaders to Walk Out". Newsweek. Accessed April 7, 2017._http://www.newsweek.com/uganda-museveni-prompts-western-leaders-walkout-icc-useless-459605.

Geissel, Brigitte, Marianne Kneuer, & Hans-Joachim Lauth (2016). "Measuring the quality of Democracy: Introduction", *The International Political Science Review,* 37(5): 571-580.

Goldin, Ian (2013). *Divided Nations: Why Global Governance is Failing and What Can be Done About It,* Oxford, Oxford University Press.

Green, Duncan (2016). *How Change Happens*, Oxford, Oxford University Press.
Hanhimäki, Jussi M. (2015). *The United Nations: A Very Short Guide,* Oxford University Press.
Hoge, Warren (2005). "U.N. Condemns Zimbabwe for Bulldozing Urban Slums". New York Times. Accessed April 7, 2017._http://www.nytimes.com/2005/07/23/world/africa/un-condemns-zimbabwe-for-bulldozing-urban-slums.html?_r=0.
Human Rights Watch (2002). News: "International Criminal Court a Reality: Human Rights Watch Applauds Historic Justice Benchmark". Accessed April 7, 2017._https://www.hrw.org/news/2002/04/11/international-criminal-court-reality.
ILO 2015. *Global Employment Trends for Youth.* Accessed April 7, 2017._http://www.ilo.org/wcmsp5/groups/public/---dgreports/---dcomm/---publ/documents/publication/wcms_412015.pdf.
ILO 2016. *Women at Work. Trends 2016.* Accessed April 7, 2017._http://www.ilo.org/wcmsp5/groups/public/---dgreports/---dcomm/---publ/documents/publication/wcms_457317.pdf.
International Commission on Intervention and State Sovereignty (2001). *The Responsibility to Protect,* Ottawa.
Inter-Parliamentary Union 2016. *Youth participation in national parliaments.* Accessed April 7, 2017._http://www.ipu.org/pdf/publications/youthrep-e.pdf.
Jolly, Richard, Louis Emmerij and Thomas Weiss (2005). *The Power of UN Ideas,* City University of New York.
Jonah, James O.C. (2007). 'Secretariat: Independence and Reform', in Weiss & Daws, op.cit.
Keane, John (2003). *Global Civil Society,* Cambridge, Cambridge University Press.
Knight A.W. (2002). "The Future of the UN Security Council" in Andrew Cooper et al. *Enhancing Global Governance,* Tokyo, United Nations University Press.
Langille, Peter (2015). "Team UN, world police: why we need an emergency peace service", The Conversation. Accessed April 7, 2017. http://theconversation.com/team-un-world-police-why-we-need-an-emergency-peace-service-42491.
Lee, Rachel (2007). *The Jericho Pact,* Don Mills, Ontario, MIRA Books.
Lu, Catherine (2006). "World Government", *Stanford Encyclopedia of Philosophy,* Stanford Calif., Stanford University Press.
Luck, Edward C. (2015). 'R2P at Ten: A New Mindset for a New Era?', *Global Governance,* 21(4):499-504.
Luck, Edward C. (2003). *Reforming the United Nations: Lessons from a History in Progress,* New Haven, Academic Council on the United Nations System.
Lyons, F.S.L. (1963). *Internationalism in Europe: 1815-1914,* Leiden, A.W. Sijthoff.
MacMillan, Margaret (2002). *Paris 1919,* New York, Random House Paperbacks.
Malone, David (2007). 'Security Council', in Weiss & Daws, op.cit.
Mani, Rama (2007). 'Peaceful Settlement of Disputes and Conflict Prevention', in Weiss & Daws, op.cit.
Mazower, Mark (2013). *Governing the World: The History of an Idea, 1815 to the Present,* New York, Penguin Books.
Meacham, Jon (2003). *Franklin and Winston,* New York, Random House.
Monbiot, George (2016). *How Did We Get Into this Mess?* London, Verso.
Murphy, C. N. (1994). *International Organization and Industrial Change: Global Governance Since 1850,* Cambridge, Polity Press.
Newman, Edward (2007). Secretary-General, in Weiss & Daws, op.cit.
Obenland, Wolfgang (2016). *Options for Strengthening Global Tax Governance,* Bonn, Friedrich-Ebert Stiftung.
Ochieng, Lilian (2016). "M-Pesa subscribers outside Kenya increase to 6m". Business Daily Africa. Accessed April 7, 2017._http://www.businessdailyafrica.com/Corporate-News/M-Pesa-subscribers-outside-Kenya-increase-to-6m/-/539550/3177986/-/6mar53z/-/index.html.

OECD. Development Finance Data. Accessed April 7, 2017. http://www.oecd.org/dac/stats/data.htm.

OECD (2006). *International Migrant Remittances and their Role in Development.* Accessed April 7, 2017. http://www.oecd.org/els/mig/38840502.pdf.

PBS Frontline. "The Spread of Zika". Accessed April 7, 2017. http://apps.frontline.org/zika/.

Piketty, Thomas (2015). *The Economics of Inequality,* Cambridge Mass, the Belknap Press of Harvard University Press.

Plesch, Dan and Thomas G. Weiss (2015). "1945's Lesson: 'Good Enough' Global Governance Ain't Good Enough", *Global Governance,* 21(2).

Ramcharan, Bertrand G. (2011). *The UN Human Rights Council,* Global Institutions series, Oxon/New York, Routledge.

Reimagining the Future: Towards Democratic Governance (2000). La Trobe University, Australia, Toda Institute, Japan, Focus on Global South, Thailand.

Reinalda, Bob (2001). *International Conferences at the Heart of International Organizations,* Canterbury, European Consortium for Political Research.

Reinalda, Bob (2003). *The Evolution of Public and Private International Organizations Before 1919,* Paper prepared for the 19th World Congress of the International Political Science Association, Durban, South Africa.

Rixen, Thomas (2011). "Global Tax Governance", *Global Governance.*

Roche, Douglas (2015). *The United Nations in the 21st Century,* Toronto, James Lorimer.

Roser, Max and Esteban Ortiz-Ospina (2017). 'Global Extreme Poverty'. Published online at OurWorldInData.org. Accessed April 7, 2017. https://ourworldindata.org/extreme-poverty/.

Rothkopf, David (2008). *Superclass,* New York, Penguin.

Rudd, Kevin the Hon. (2016). *UN 2030: Rebuilding Order in a Fragmenting World,* Chair's Report, Independent Commission on Multilateralism, New York, International Peace Institute.

Sanchez, Raf (2016). "Turkey forces aid group Mercy Corps to shut down its operations". New York Times. Accessed April 7, 2017. http://www.telegraph.co.uk/news/2017/03/08/turkey-forces-aid-group-mercy-corps-shut-operations/.

Saudi Press Agency (2016). "Ambassador Al-Moallami: Re-electing the Kingdom as Member of the Human Rights Council Reflects the International Community's Trust". Accessed April 7, 2017. http://www.spa.gov.sa/viewstory.php?lang=en&newsid=1553296.

Schemeil, Yves (2003). "Expertise and Politics: Consensus Making within the World Bank and the World Meteorological Association", in Bob Reinalda & Bertjan Verbeek (eds.) *Decision-Making in International Organizations,* London, Routledge.

Schlesinger, Stephen C. (2003). *Act of Creation: The Founding of the United Nations,* New York, Westview Press.

Schwartzberg, Joseph E. (2013). *Transforming the United Nations System: Designs for a Workable World,* Tokyo, United Nations University Press.

SDG Fund website. Accessed April 7, 2017. http://www.sdgfund.org/.

Senate Select Committee on Intelligence (2014). "Committee Study of the Central Intelligence Agency's Detention and Interrogation Program". Accessed April 7, 2017. http://www.intelligence.senate.gov/sites/default/files/press/findings-and-conclusions.pdf.

Sieff, Kevin (2016). "Gambia is the latest African country deciding to pull out of International Criminal Court". Washington Post. Accessed April 7, 2017. https://www.washingtonpost.com/world/gambia-latest-african-country-deciding-to-pull-out-of-international-criminal-court/2016/10/26/7f54d068-c4ca-440f-848f-e211ba29dc34_story.html.

Smith, Michael G. (2016). 'Review of the UN High-Level Independent Panel on Peace Operations: Uniting Our Strengths for Peace: Politics, Partnerships and People', in *Global Governance* 22 (2): 179-187.

South Centre (1996). *For a Strong and Democratic United Nations: A South Perspective on United Nations Reform,* Geneva, the South Centre.
Tapscott, Don (2014). "A Bretton Woods for the 21st Century". Harvard Business Review. Accessed April 7, 2017. https://hbr.org/2014/03/a-bretton-woods-for-the-21st-century.
Trent, John E. (2007). *Modernizing the United Nations System: Civil Society's Role in Moving from International Relations to Global Governance,* Opladen, Barbara Budrich Publishers.
UBUNTU (2004). "Proposals for the Reform of the System of International Institutions: Future Scenarios", Barcelona, Technical University of Catalonia. Accessed April 7, 2017. http://www.ubuntu.org/pdf/seminari_eng.pdf.
United Nations (1960). *Declaration on the Granting of Independence to Colonial Countries and Peoples.* Accessed April 7, 2017. http://www.un.org/en/decolonization/declaration.shtml.
United Nations (1987). Report of the World Commission on Environment and Development: Our Common Future. Accessed April 7, 2017. http://www.un-documents.net/our-common-future.pdf.
United Nations (2012). Independent Evaluation of Delivering as One. Main Report. Accessed April 7, 2017. http://www.un.org/en/ga/deliveringasone/pdf/summaryreportweb.pdf.
United Nations (2013). Press Release: Secretary-General Statement. "Culture, Religion, Tradition Can Never Justify Denial of Rights, Secretary-General Stresses in Message to Conference on Sexual Orientation, Gender Identity". Accessed April 7, 2017. http://www.un.org/press/en/2013/sgsm14944.doc.htm.
United Nations (2013). A Million Voices: the World We Want. Accessed April 7, 2017. http://www.ohchr.org/Documents/Issues/MDGs/UNDGAMillionVoices.pdf.
United Nations (2015). Sustainable Development blog post: "UN Secretary-General's initiative aims to strengthen climate resilience of the world's most vulnerable countries and people". Accessed April 7, 2017. http://www.un.org/sustainabledevelopment/blog/2015/11/un-secretary-generals-initiative-aims-to-strengthen-climate-resilience-of-the-worlds-most-vulnerable-countries-and-people/.
United Nations (2016). "Opening remarks: High Level Thematic Debate on Peace and Security". Accessed April 7, 2017. http://www.un.org/pga/70/2016/05/10/opening-remarks-high-level-thematic-debate-on-peace-and-security/.
United Nations Educational, Scientific and Cultural Organization (UNESCO), Global Education First Initiative (GEFI). Accessed April 7, 2017. http://www.unesco.org/new/en/gefi/partnerships/.
United Nations High Commissioner for Refugees (UNHCR 2014). "Statement by António Guterres, United Nations High Commissioner for Refugees, Third Committee of the General Assembly, 69th Session, 5 November 2014". Accessed April 7, 2017. http://www.unhcr.org/admin/hcspeeches/545b36759/statement-antonio-guterres-united-nations-high-commissioner-refugees-third.html.
United Nations High Commissioner for Refugees (UNHCR 2017). "Syria Emergency". Accessed April 7, 2017. http://www.unhcr.org/syria-emergency.html.
United Nations Human Rights Council (UNHRC 2017). "Human rights abuses and international humanitarian law violations in the Syrian Arab Republic, 21 July 2016—28 February 2017". A/HCR/34/CPR.3 on 10 March 2017. Accessed April 7, 2017. http://www.ohchr.org/EN/HRBodies/HRC/IICISyria/Pages/IndependentInternationalCommission.aspx.
United Nations Information Service Vienna (UN Information Service). "United Nations in General". Accessed April 7, 2017. http://www.unis.unvienna.org/unis/en/topics/selection_secretary-general.html.
United Nations Office of the High Commissioner for Human Rights (UN OHCHR 2016). "Zeid's Global Human Rights Update". Accessed April 7, 2017. http://www.ohchr.org/EN/NewsEvents/Pages/GlobalHumanRightsUpdate.aspx.

United Nations Research Institute for Social Development (UNRISD 2015). Matthew Martin. "Beyond Addis: How Can We Finance the SDGs?" Accessed April 7, 2017._http://www.unrisd.org/UNRISD/web-site/newsview.nsf/(httpNews)/4F6F18839672DBEEC1257EBA004314A5?OpenDocument.

United Nations Secretariat (2015). Report of the Secretary-General. Implementation of General Assembly Resolution 67/226 on the quadrennial comprehensive policy review of operational activities for development of the United Nations system (QCPR). Accessed April 7, 2017. http://www.un.org/en/ecosoc/qcpr/pdf/sg_report_on_qcpr_adv_2015.pdf.

United Nations Secretary-General (UNSG 2013). Secretary-General's address to the General Assembly on 22 January 2013. Accessed April 7, 2017._https://www.un.org/sg/en/content/sg/statement/2013-01-22/secretary-generals-address-general-assembly.

United Nations Secretary-General (UNSG 2013). Secretary-General's remarks at High-Level Event on Supporting Civil Society, delivered on 23 September 2013. Accessed April 7, 2017. https://www.un.org/sg/en/content/sg/statement/2013-09-23/secretary-generals-remarks-high-level-event-supporting-civil-society.

United Nations Secretary-General (UNSG 2016). Secretary-General's remarks at Columbia University Commencement, delivered on 18 May 2016. Accessed April 7, 2017. https://www.un.org/sg/en/content/sg/statement/2016-05-18/secretary-generals-remarks-columbia-university-commencement-prepared.

United States Institute of Peace. "Confronting Crimes Against Humanity". Accessed April 7, 2017. http://www.usip.org/sites/default/files/file/09sg.pdf.

Volt, Jonathan (2015). "Opinion: Why does United Nations Secretary-General insist on placing Public-Private Partnerships in the heart of the Post 2015 Development Agenda?"_Earth System Governance. Accessed April 7, 2017. http://sdg.earthsystemgovernance.org/sdg/news/2015-03-19/opinion-why-does-united-nations-secretary-general-insist-placing-public-private-part.

Waltz, Kenneth N. (1965). *Man, the State and War,* New York, Columbia University Press.

Weiss, Thomas and Sam Daws (eds.) (2007). *The Oxford Handbook of the United Nations,* Oxford, Oxford University Press.

Weiss, Thomas G., David P. Forsythe, Roger A. Coate and Kelly-Kate Pease (2014). *The UN and Changing World Politics* 7th Edition, Westview Press.

Weiss, Thomas G. (2009). *What's Wrong with the United Nations and How to Fix It?* Cambridge, Polity Press.

Weiss, Thomas G. (2011). *Thinking about Global Governance: Why People and Ideas Matter,* Oxon/New York, Routledge.

Weiss, Thomas G. (2014a). *Governing the World,* Boulder, Paradigm Publishers.

Weiss, Thomas G. (2014b). "After Syria, Whither R2P?". E-International Relations. Accessed April 7, 2017._http://www.e-ir.info/2014/02/02/after-syria-whither-r2p/.

Wells. H.G. (1933) *The Shape of Things to Come,* Gutenberg Project electronic book.

Wendt, Alexander (2003). "Why a World State is Inevitable", *European Journal of International Relations.*

World Bank. "The World Bank Group and the United Nations: Working Together for Development". Accessed April 7, 2017._http://www.un.org/esa/ffd/ffd3/wp-content/uploads/sites/2/WBG-UN-Brochure.pdf.

World Bank (2015). Press release. "International Migration at All-Time High". Accessed April 7, 2017. http://www.worldbank.org/en/news/press-release/2015/12/18/international-migrants-and-remittances-continue-to-grow-as-people-search-for-better-opportunities-new-report-finds.

World Court of Human Rights. World Court of Human Rights Development Project, The Case for Support. Accessed April 7, 2017._http://www.worldcourtofhumanrights.net/project-overview.

World Food Programme (WFP 2014). News: "For 64 Million People, It's A Dollar, For 1.7 Million Syrian Refugees It's A Lifeline". Accessed April 7, 2017. https://www.wfp.org/news/news-release/64-million-people-its-dollar-17-million-syrian-refugees-its-lifeline.

World Health Organization (2015). Report of the Ebola Interim Assessment Panel. July 2015. Accessed April 7, 2017. http://www.who.int/csr/resources/publications/ebola/report-by-panel.pdf?ua=1.

Youth Envoy website. Accessed April 7, 2017. http://www.un.org/youthenvoy/about/.

Index

www.ingramcontent.com/pod-product-compliance
Lightning Source LLC
LaVergne TN
LVHW082339200926
848481LV00012B/3391
* 9 7 8 1 0 1 3 2 9 4 9 8 3 *